Waterways in the Making

Edward Paget-Tomlinson

CanalBookShop

Cover illustration:
January 1996. A replacement tail gate is being fitted to the bottom lock of the Tardebigge flight of the
Worcester and Birmingham Canal. With its thirty locks, this is the longest flight in the country.

The method of canal cutting shown here was called benching and was widely used. Spoil was transferred to the bank in stages; from the bed of the canal to a "bench" or shelf half way up the sides - and thence from that bench to the top of the bank, from where it could be carted away.

Waterways in the Making

Written and illustrated by
Edward Paget-Tomlinson

CanalBookShop

Waterways in the Making

Edward Paget-Tomlinson

First edition published by The Landscape Press, 1996

Second edition published 2019 by

CanalBookShop
Audlem Mill Limited The Wharf Audlem Cheshire CW3 0DX
www.canalbookshop.co.uk

ISBN 978-0-9955180-9-4

CONTENTS

INTRODUCTION   7

FROM RIVERS TO NAVIGATIONS   8
Early river navigations
Mills and the competition for water
River improvement and lock development
Weirs
The navigable drains

CUTTING THE CANALS   21
Planning and surveying
Pegging out
Digging and puddling
Protecting the banks

ACROSS THE VALLEY AND UNDER
THE HILL   38
Aqueducts
Tunnels

CHANGING THE LEVEL   52
Locks
Inclined planes
Canal lifts

CROSSING THE WATERWAY   74
Fixed bridges
Lift bridges
Swing bridges

ALONG THE TOWPATH   84
Maintaining the towpath
Mileposts and stiles
Horse towing features

WATER SUPPLY   90
Water requirements
Water supply and control
Reservoirs, rivers and pumps

MAINTAINING THE NAVIGATIONS   98
Weed control
Dredging
Breaches
Lock and tunnel maintenance
Ice breaking

NEW BEGINNINGS   110
Waterway recovery and restoration
Amenity and recreation

TOOLS OF THE TRADE   114

BIBLIOGRAPHY   116

ACKNOWLEDGEMENTS   118

INDEX   119

DEDICATION

by the author in the first edition, 1996

To the staff at British Waterways, past and present, and to their colleagues
at the National Waterways Museum at Gloucester whose help and
encouragement have made this book possible.

PUBLISHERS NOTE

to the second edition, 2019

The author, Edward Paget-Tomlinson, died in 2003. This edition is as written by him, save for a few updates by Peter Silvester to reflect some changes in the 20+ years since first publication in 1996. It has been published by CanalBookShop, who have also reprinted the author's 2004 book "Colours of the Cut", and have published posthumously a new book of his drawings of the BCN, "The A-Z of the Birmingham Canal Navigations", with historical notes by Ray Shill.

INTRODUCTION

Today, with the accent so rightly on the waterways as an amenity, their origins and initial purposes are in danger of being forgotten. In words and pictures, but with an emphasis on the pictures, this book aims to explain the background to the features and equipment the boater is bound to see when travelling a waterway; aqueducts, locks and tunnels, obviously - but also bridges and weirs, culverts, towpath stiles and railings and many other small items so easily overlooked. The choice of drawings rather than photographs is deliberate because they can be composed to illustrate a precise point and angled to suit the layout of the page, achieving viewpoints denied to the camera -as well as portraying scenes that pre-date the camera itself.

The overall theme is the creation of the navigable waterways system of England and Wales - from the early river improvements to the later canals - all from the technical perspective. While penetrating studies have been made, and no doubt will continue to be made, on the economics of the rivers and canals - this work leaves out all the problems of finance and legislation and discusses instead the planning and construction, the engineering features, the maintenance and the supply of water; in short the physical aspects that go to make up the waterways themselves.

Space has demanded concentration on England and Wales although Scotland and Ireland and, above all the continent of Europe, have much to offer of engineering merit. There is no room here to discuss the marvels of European waterways, or to consider the canals of Scotland in detail - albeit the concept and execution of the Caledonian Canal is magnificent, while the contribution the Forth & Clyde made to the industrial economy of central Scotland cannot be overestimated. Ireland's waterways were built to open up the country, and like the Caledonian, were government backed and built on a massive scale. It was otherwise in England and Wales where almost the whole system - the Royal Military Canal being an exception - was privately financed. This meant economy of construction and notably in the choice of gauge. The resulting narrow canal system is peculiarly English and the narrow boat has come to symbolize the English canals, but where possible canals were built to broader dimensions to take those craft that were already plying the local river navigations.

This book considers the construction and maintenance of both types of waterway, from the improvements made to rivers in order to increase their navigability, through to the purpose built canals that followed them.

FROM RIVERS TO NAVIGATIONS

When planning a holiday on a waterway, people tend to think in terms of man made canals, but often part of their route will be a river; not an untamed torrent but a placid navigation. This was the achievement of the river improvers of the seventeenth and eighteenth centuries; although the longest river of England and Wales - the Severn - because of its peculiar hazards, had to wait until the nineteenth century to be tamed, and even today is not exactly placid. Likewise the River Trent was not made into a really effective navigation until the 1920s.

Many rivers were always navigable, certainly up to the limits of the tide. The Severn was a notable case; naturally navigable, although with difficulty, not only to the tidal limit of Worcester, but because of the volume of land water draining down its route, sometimes to just short of Welshpool; an amazing 160 miles or so from its confluence with the River Avon at Bristol. A little physical improvement to some rivers could speedily increase their navigability. Beginning at the tidal limit of Knottingley, early work on the Aire and the Calder started in May 1699, and resulted in a boat reaching Wakefield in December of the same year, and further still to Leeds at the end of the following one. The Calder line was not properly completed until 1702, while the route to Leeds, with the help of a length of artificial cut, was not completed until 1709.

East Anglia was a choice area for river improvement with the twin aims of drainage and navigation; of these the former predominating. There were three main periods of work, intertwined with political and economic events; 1662-1665 following the Civil War, 1697-1700 preceding the wars with France and 1719-1721 before the South Sea Company crash. There had been still earlier efforts in Warwickshire on the River Avon. William Sandys had improved it up to Stratford for 30 ton craft by 1639. Further east, on the Great Ouse, boats could come within 7.5 miles of Bedford by 1635.

So how was all of this achieved?

Unimproved until the mid nineteenth century, the River Severn was most readily navigable in flood conditions, although the fierce current made passage upstream difficult. A major obstacle was lack of a towing path for horses. This was remedied in stages, starting in 1772 and completed in 1812, by when there was a horse path from Shrewsbury to Gloucester, run by a series of horse path companies. The bow haulers seen in the illustration *below*, stumbled along the bank on a path made and maintained by their own usage.

They were eventually to be put out of business by the new organisation and its use of horses for towing; the first instance of improvement of the river.

The vessel seen labouring her way upstream is an upriver square rigged trow which could be sailed when wind and current served; but she would have had to lower her sail for the bridges such as that at Bewdley. There were few others across the Severn in the eighteenth century.

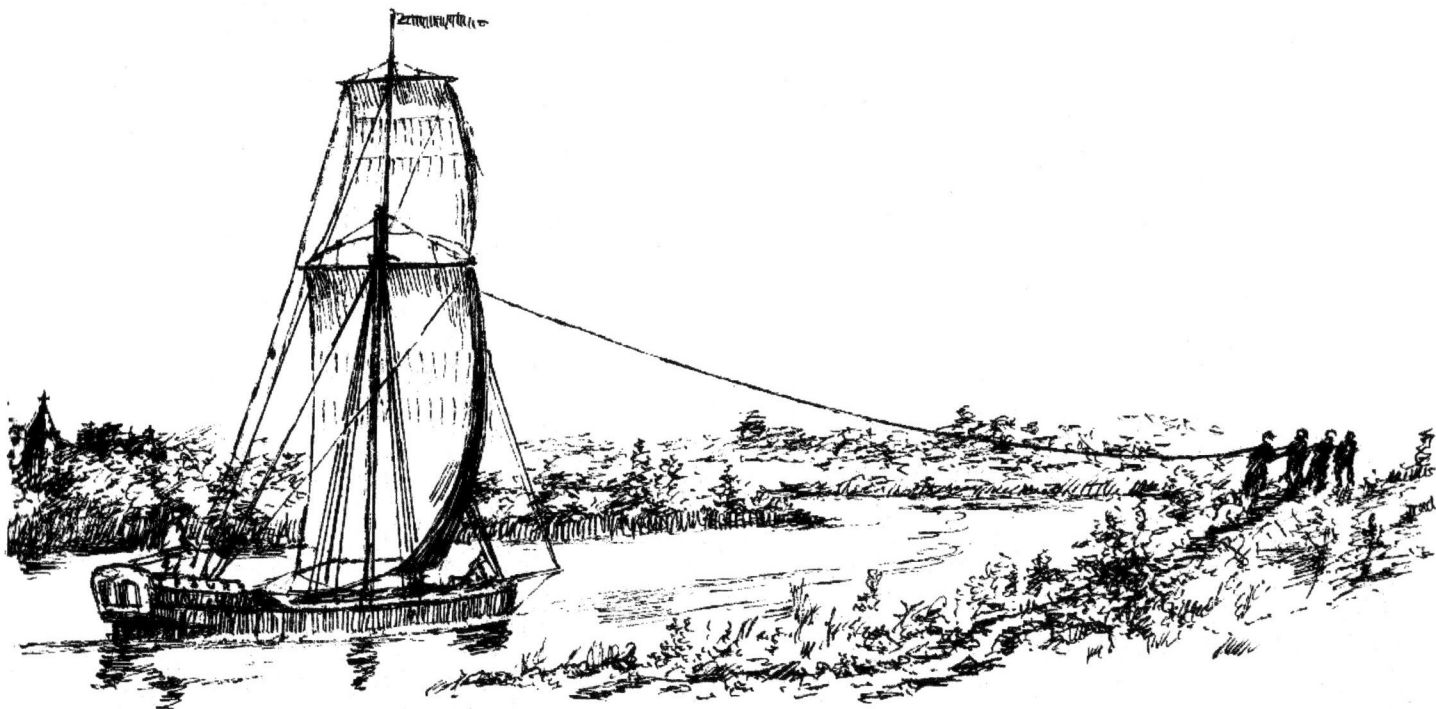

MILLS AND THE COMPETITION FOR WATER

Improving a river for navigation was frequently hampered by the existence of weirs: weirs used to trap fish and weirs used to provide a head of water for mill wheels. In centuries when meat was scarce and sea fish unobtainable inland, freshwater fish was a vital part of the diet - quite apart from the ordinances laid down by the Church. They were caught by various types of trap and an example from the River Boyne in Ireland is illustrated *top right;* in this case for salmon. When the fish pass upstream between the converging grids, they find themselves in a chamber from which there is no escape. Built across a river, such a fish weir effectively stopped navigation - although as an obstacle it might only be an affair of stakes and basketwork, or simply of nets.

More permanent and substantial however were the mill dams. These provided a reservoir for watermills, and incidentally doubled as fishponds providing more income for the millers. To allow boats to pass through these dams, they had to be pierced by a lock of some sort - of which more later. Virtually all river improvements were hindered by mills and millers, and the illustration *centre left* shows a boat aground below a mill. Such problems were not surprising as the passage of a

boat through the locks would reduce the water supply to the wheel, and at the same time raise the level below the weir or dam and choke the wheel's tail race.

Design of the waterwheel determined the height of the weir, and an undershot wheel illustrated *centre right* needed the least head of water, a breast shot wheel bottom right where the leat comes just above the wheel's centre would need more water, while an overshot wheel bottom *left* illustration would need more still.

River improvement was contemporary with a growing industrialisation dependent almost entirely on water power, not only used for milling grain but for driving sawmills, forge bellows, trip hammers, fulling stocks, gunpowder mills, and later spinning frames, mules and looms. No wonder the antagonism between the navigators and the millers was deep - although eventually it was usually overcome by local agreements.

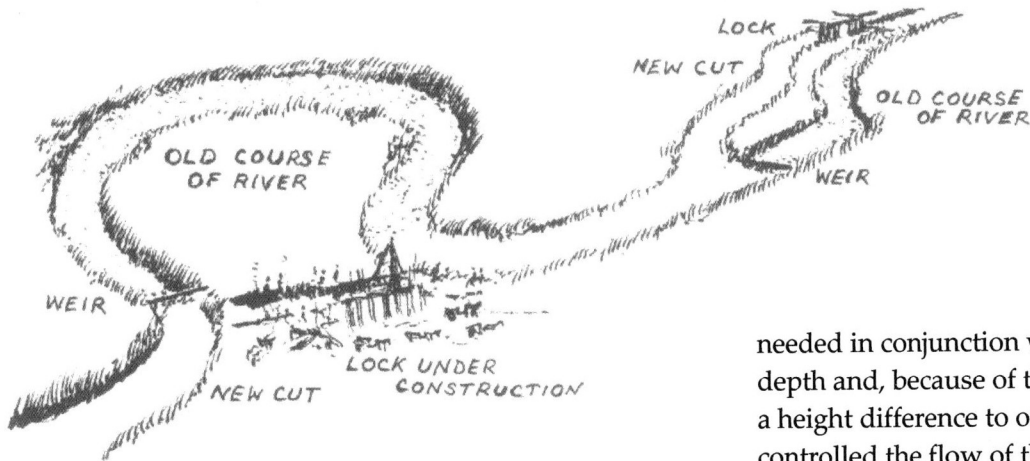

OLD COURSE OF RIVER

LOCK

NEW CUT

OLD COURSE OF RIVER

WEIR

WEIR

NEW CUT

LOCK UNDER CONSTRUCTION

In spite of such obstructions, improvement went ahead. The improvers - or undertakers as they often were known - had to take account of the twin liabilities of drought and flood, of rainfall, the number and size of tributaries and the natural fall of the river, which could be considerable in hilly country. The River Calder in the West Riding, for example, dropped nearly 40 metres in 24 miles. Adequate depth was the first consideration, achieved by holding back the water by means of weirs passable by locks. Granted the millers needed water for their own purposes, but a navigation demanded separate weirs of its own to control such depth; these were used in conjunction with channel straightening by artificial cuts.

The River Wey in Surrey was an early achievement, being made navigable to Guildford by 1653. The illustration *above* shows a length in panorama with two bends bypassed by cuts, each with a lock at its lower or tail end. These were needed in conjunction with the weirs to maintain depth and, because of the fall of the river, also had a height difference to overcome. The weirs controlled the flow of the original stream. Tampering with nature did however create problems; the cuts checked the current and so encouraged shoals, while the natural stream tended to deposit silt across the tail of the artificial cut. This the locks were supposed to clear, by the scour of water released by the paddles; a reason for siting them at the tails of the cuts.

The illustration *below* shows how rivers could be improved to contain floodwater, by building up floodbanks well back from the channel, creating washlands which could be allowed to flood. In effect the rivers were given a wider course to follow. This was standard East Anglian practice.

FLOOD BANK   WASHLANDS   FLOODBANK

Current, especially in flood conditions, erodes river banks, while the wash of powered craft creates added damage. Ever since river improvements were started, bank protection has, therefore, been a priority: methods can include a simple revetment of piles backed by stones as in the illustration *upper left,* or more costly stone pitching *bottom left* illustration, which if built vertically can increase the cross sectional area of the water, making passage easier. The *upper right hand* illustration shows work on the Little Ouse, and the *bottom right hand* illustration the modern use of camp shedding (or camp sheeting) to build a continuous retaining wall. A line of timber piles is driven in, stiffened by kingposts at regular intervals of say 2 metre centres. Nowadays metal sheet piling has replaced timber on many jobs, but the principles of bank protection remain the same.

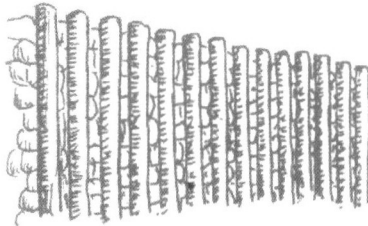

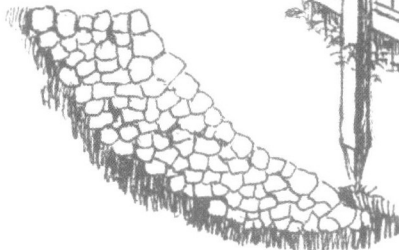

RIVER IMPROVEMENT AND LOCK DEVELOPMENT

Locks on rivers went through an evolutionary process from the primitive to the sophisticated. To pierce dams and weirs, to allow for navigation, it was simplest to make a flash lock. This was a gate which kept   water impounded behind the weir but which, when opened, released a gush or "flash" of water. This lifted the boat over the shallows and up into deeper water above. The idea was known to the Chinese before the birth of Christ and in Europe before the eleventh century. Simplest of all was a door of removable horizontal planks but an advance on this was the paddle and rimer flash lock, common on the Thames and illustrated *top left*. Removable paddles were laid against a sill in the river bed and held against the beam spanning the river by a timber framework. This doubled as a footbridge, a section (as seen here) or all of which could be swung open for a boat. The rimers with rebated sides acted as guides for the paddles and were removed in the same way. When in position the whole assembly was held tight by water pressure. To pass a boat through, the paddles and their rimers had to be drawn upwards, and if yet more depth was wanted below, more paddles could be drawn out from the fixed beam. Bigger weirs had two rows of paddles.

A flash would last an hour or so. Traffic going downstream would use it first, while the upstream boats would wait until the upper and lower sections of water (i.e. above and below the flash lock) were nearly level and would then be warped through by a windlass on the bank. Immediately the traffic had passed, the lock was closed in order to build up water for the next arrivals.

Watergates, an example is shown *bottom left*, were an improvement. They were complete gates with the paddles either incorporated into the gate or into a fixed weir alongside. They were found in the Midlands, the West Country and East Anglia. Intended purely for navigation, they did not hinder mills as they were left open until a boat appeared. Two lasted on the Warwickshire Avon until the 1950s. Illustrated is that at Pensham near Pershore. The weir sluices are on the left. Watergates were slow to work because they could not be opened until water levels were equal on either side and this depended on the closure of another watergate below, maybe some miles away. A winch was needed to open such a horizontally swinging gate, as seen here.

East Anglian watergates were called staunches. They were worked in essentially the same way, except that the vertical gates were lifted against the head of water by walking up the 2 metre diameter wheel. These gates could also act as a paddle or sluice, although there were usually sluices alongside. Remains of such a staunch survived at Bottisham near Cambridge certainly until 1969. The illustration *upper right*, shows this staunch in action, the gate being raised to allow a Fens lighter to pass through. A detail of its winding gear is shown *below*.

Pound locks eventually replaced flash locks at mill and navigation weirs and became the type in most general use from the seventeenth century onwards.

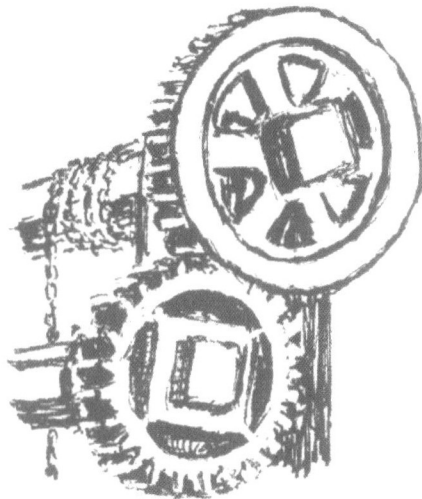

Instead of a single gate or staunch separating two different sections of the navigation, a pound lock depends upon a volume of water being impounded in a chamber by a set of upper and lower gates. Boats using such pound locks pass from one section of the waterway to another via this chamber, entering and leaving through the containing gates. Any flow of water that needs to by-pass the lock chamber does so in its own parallel channel. The illustration *lower right* shows such a pound lock on the river navigation at Keynsham on the Bristol Avon. The natural channel of the river continues upstream to the right of the lock.

Cuts made to improve river navigations have to be protected from floods. This is done by building an extra lock, or at least a pair of gates, at the head of the cut, with the change of level lock at the tail. Normally a flood lock or gate is left open, only being closed in flood conditions. Closure of a flood gate also closes the navigation, but a flood lock can pass traffic. Whereas most flood locks have mitred gates at top and bottom, some in East Anglia have a dual role with guillotine gates acting as sluices, and able to be raised against a head of water.

Weirs, by which a river's depth is maintained, have already been mentioned. Fixed weirs are just that, i.e. without the means of adjustment. Moveable weirs, in contrast, have doors which control the flow over the sills. Illustrated *below left* is a fixed overfall weir on the River Severn; "overfall" because the water flows over the sill on its crest. To increase the rate of discharge over the weir, the crest was built at an angle to the flow of water in order to lengthen it. With piles used to anchor the rubble built structure, the design provides a steep slope on the upstream side and a gentler one downstream to reduce the force of the water's flow. Downstream slopes are either smooth aprons of dressed stone, as illustrated, or they may be stepped. To increase sill length, some weirs are built V shaped, while others have been given a curve, like the Horseshoe Falls on the Dee above Llangollen.

Moveable weirs or sluices are varied in design, but normally have vertically rising gates or doors. The illustration *below right* shows that at Dutton on the River Weaver in Cheshire.

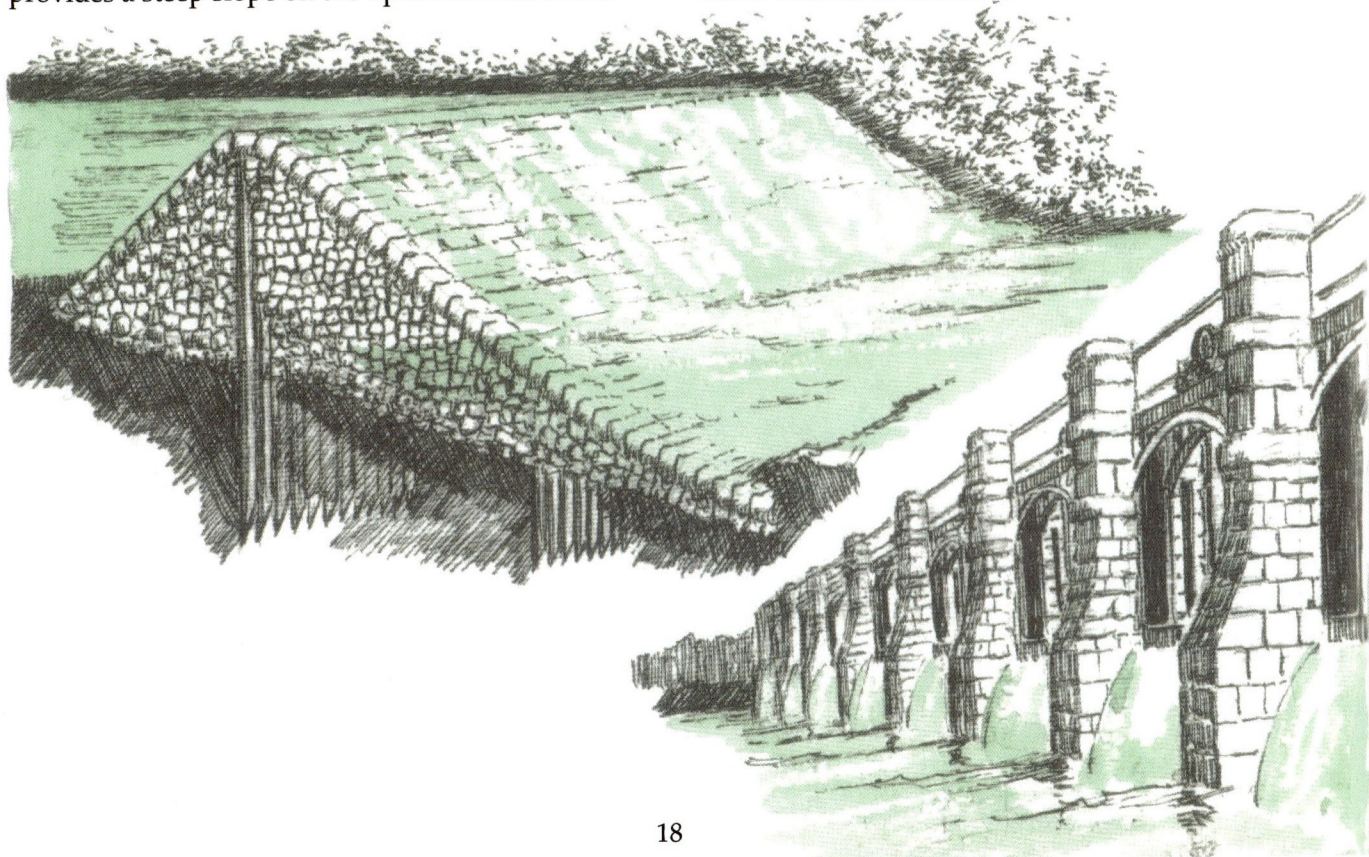

18

The waterways maps show a number of navigable drains - especially in the east of the country. By their very name these show the priority that they give to drainage over navigation.

Floods are the enemy of land drainage, and in East Anglia in particular flood control takes precedence. Indeed there is a conflict here, because navigations need improved and deeper water-ways, which by their nature increase the risk of flood. In contrast, riparian owners, with summer crops at risk, want lower water levels. Keeping farmland drained and free of floodwater has been an ongoing task since the seventeenth century, when Cornelius Vermuyden drained the Fens. He also worked on Hatfield Chase, north east of Doncaster, while other engineers carried out similar drainage works elsewhere. The Somerset levels, the Fylde of Lancashire, the mosses of Shropshire and the marshes of Sussex all saw such activity. In every case the main task was to pass the landwater seaward by new channels, and to check the ingress of the tide. The Fens demanded a whole network of cut channels. These are dominated by the two Bedford Rivers feeding into the Ouse and linked with the waterways of the Middle Level centred on the Nene. The major obstacle to success was the tide which backed up the landwater and deposited silt. Vermuyden

solved this by building the sluice at Denver so that the tide could be turned up the New Bedford or Hundred Foot River (so named after its original width) while allowing landwater to pass down the Great Ouse to the Wash. The panoramic map overleaf shows some of this area. The Old Bedford River was completed in 1637, the Hundred Foot in 1651.

To lift water from channel to channel or from the field drains to the river requires pumps - powered by wind, steam, diesel or electricity. The illustration *below* shows the wind powered Herringfleet drainage mill on the River Waveney in Suffolk. Effectively it is a water-wheel in reverse, scooping up water and lifting it upwards for 2 metres to a higher drainage channel.

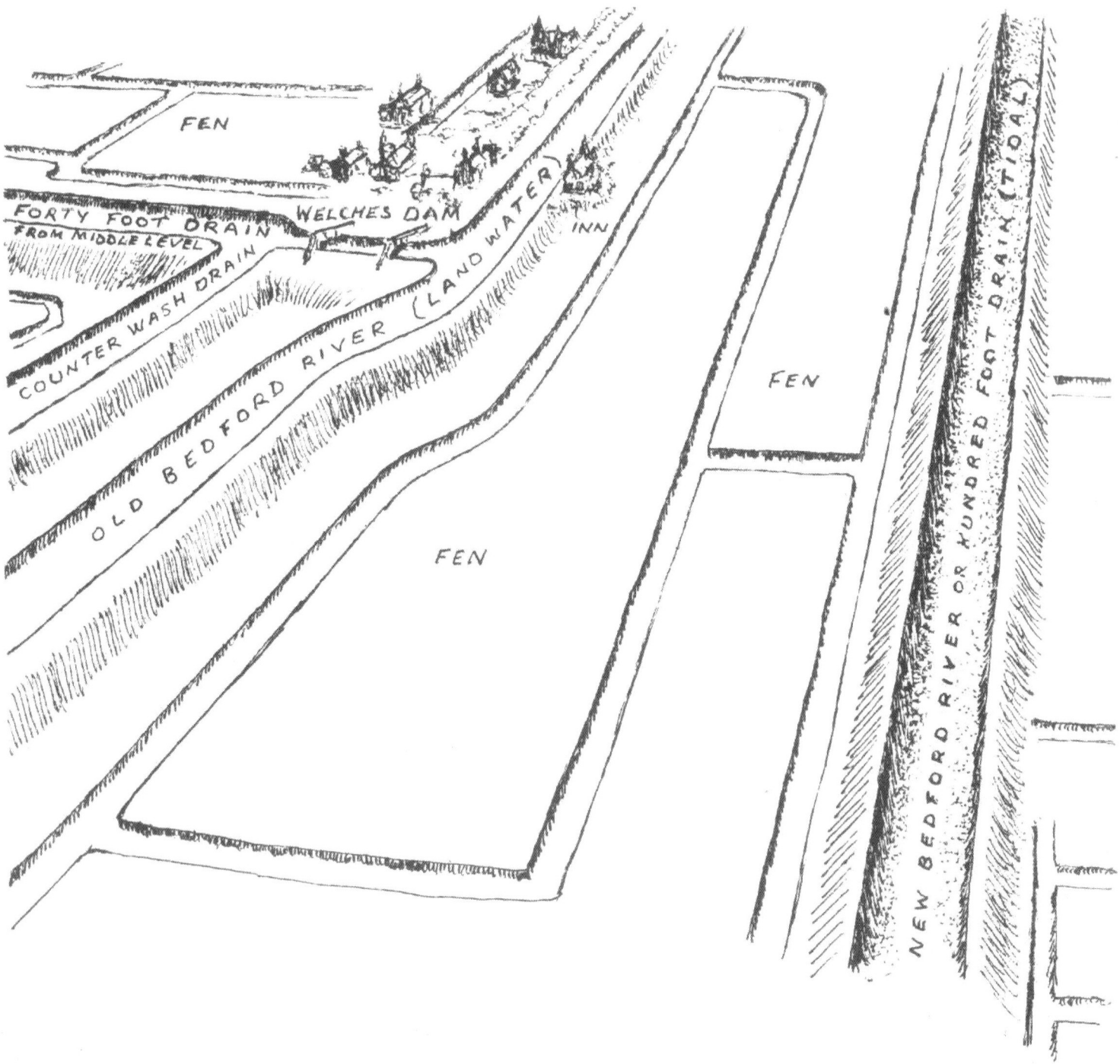

FEN

FORTY FOOT DRAIN
FROM MIDDLE LEVEL

WELCHES DAM

COUNTER WASH DRAIN

OLD BEDFORD RIVER (LAND WATER)

INN

FEN

FEN

FEN

NEW BEDFORD RIVER OR HUNDRED FOOT DRAIN (TIDAL)

CUTTING THE CANALS

River improvement demanded the digging of artificial cuts but the idea of an entirely man made waterway was not new, even in the seventeenth century. Apart from the Roman Fossdyke, there had been a ship canal to Exeter since about 1566, while nearly half the improved River Wey was artificially cut. The pioneer Sankey Brook Navigation, opened in 1757 for some of its length, was authorized as a river improvement but ended up as a canal - so by the mid eighteenth century canal cutting was starting to become familiar.

Less familiar was the concept of a canal crossing a watershed, climbing up and down hill. There had long been such canals in Europe. The Canal du Midi was opened in 1681, and in the British Isles the Newry Canal in Ulster had provided a through route from Lough Neagh to Carlingford Lough since 1742. The Duke of Bridgewater's Canal started in 1759 as a local line to bring his coal to the Manchester market - but the extension to Runcorn and the Mersey made it part of a grander project which would demonstrate the potential of canals and their ability to join the rivers up in a national network. At the heart of this was a scheme to link the major rivers of the Mersey, Trent, Severn and Thames by a cross of canals, some of which were completed by 1777, but with the Thames link having to wait until 1790.

Once canals had proved themselves practicable, there was no stopping their builders. Watersheds were crossed from east to west and north to south. Local lines were built to bring coal and provisions to inland areas, and to carry produce outwards to markets. Following the lead of the Bridgewater Canal, cuts were dug to exploit collieries and quarries - especially limestone quarries, the lime from which was needed for soil improvement by the rapidly developing agriculture of the eighteenth century. River navigations were extended and joined by canals - and ship canals allowed the creation of inland ports.

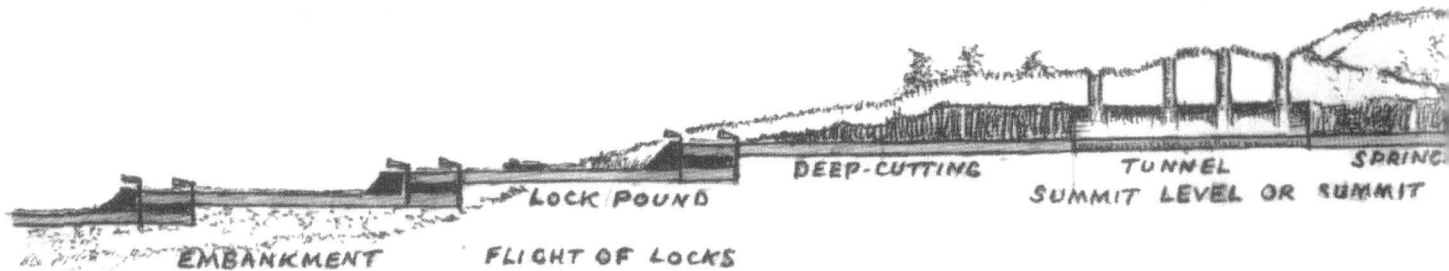

EMBANKMENT FLIGHT OF LOCKS LOCK POUND DEEP-CUTTING TUNNEL SPRING SUMMIT LEVEL OR SUMMIT

Surveying the line of canal in the eighteenth century was gruelling work, demanding hard riding. With no maps available and no precise knowledge of geological strata, the ground had to be inspected in detail and trial excavations made. Selection of gauge was a prime consideration; broad or narrow. The latter cheaper to build, the former more profitable to operate.

With the gauge established, either for 2.2 metre (7 foot) beam narrow boats or 4.3 metre (14 foot) broad craft or even for ships, the engineer's next decision was the course and length of the summit level, dependent on the availability of water. With the summit fixed, the route was worked out down to each end, the sites of locks marked and the need for cuttings, embankments, aqueducts and tunnels identified.

In planning, the central thought of the engineer, after the purpose and gauge of the canal had been decided upon, was water supply. This was not a problem when improving a river, but was essential to the success of a summit level canal as water travelled down and out of a canal with each passing boat. Ideally the main water supply should be to the summit level, fed by gravity from a reservoir, the water coming from streams, springs and land drainage. Ideally the summit level should itself be long and able to act as a reservoir. But to make it long could be an expensive business, probably involving a tunnel. In such a case the engineers had to balance the costs of a tunnel and an assured supply of water against having no tunnel but a shorter summit, and hence less water. Any summit involved some earthworks. These might include deep cuttings and excavation for locks - with embankments and aqueducts lower down, where the canal dipped to cross valleys.

These features are shown in condensed form in the illustration at the *top* of the page.

Canal design is subject to infinite variation. There might be two summits on a long line, such as on the Grand Junction Canal between London and Braunston; there might he tunnels at lower levels

22

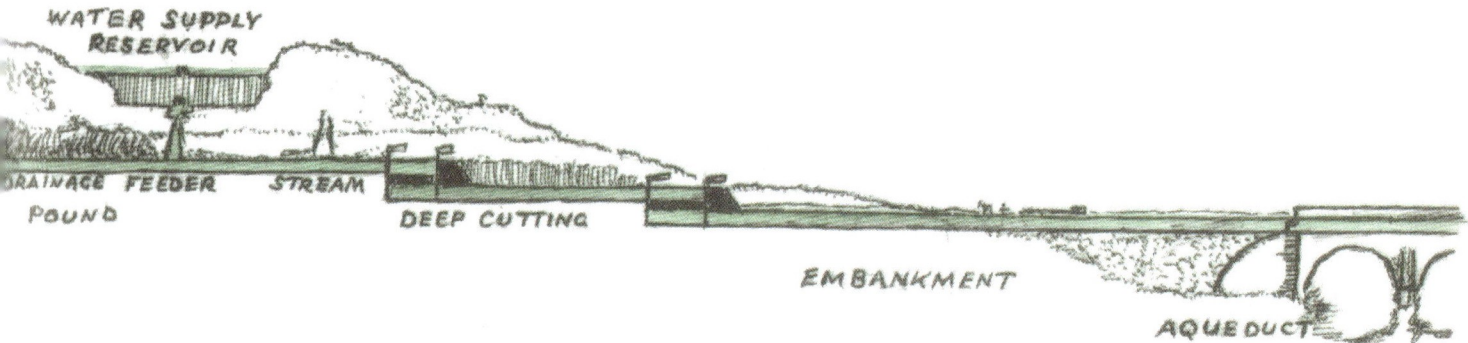

WATER SUPPLY RESERVOIR · DRAINAGE FEEDER · STREAM · POUND · DEEP CUTTING · EMBANKMENT · AQUEDUCT

as on the Trent and Mersey Canal. There might be reservoirs lower down as on the Leeds and Liverpool, while urban canal development had rules of its own, as notably shown in the Birmingham area. Here the object was to serve collieries and factories, and in later days to provide transport between factory, forge and foundry and railway goods depots. For a tight, intricate system like the Birmingham Canal Navigations, water supply was critical, largely solved by mine pumping and recirculating lockage water. The system in Nottingham followed a similar pattern although not built on different levels and being on a much smaller scale, while the London end of the Grand Junction and the Regent's Canals were a mass of docks and wharves.

This is not a study of canal acts and finance; suffice it to say that Parliamentary approval was needed for both river improvement and canal construction. This was because finance for them came from public joint stock companies, and because land would have to be compulsorily bought, streams diverted, roads crossed, water

abstracted and tolls levied for goods carried; all of which needed   Parliamentary sanction. If the canal was on private land and privately financed, no Act was needed, but this was a rare situation, one example being the Torrington Canal in Devon.

Finance for river works and canals came largely from local promoters with a stake in the success of the venture. Merchants, quarry and colliery owners, local gentry, distant investors, speculators, banks, municipal corporations and waterways engineers all wanted to see their work go ahead and so would invest. In Europe, Scotland and Ireland, state funding did take place, but in England monies were only lent to alleviate distress at the end of the Napoleonic Wars by financing works for public use. This was the task of the Exchequer Bill Loan Commissioners established in 1817. They aided the Regent's, the Gloucester and Berkeley Canals and many others.

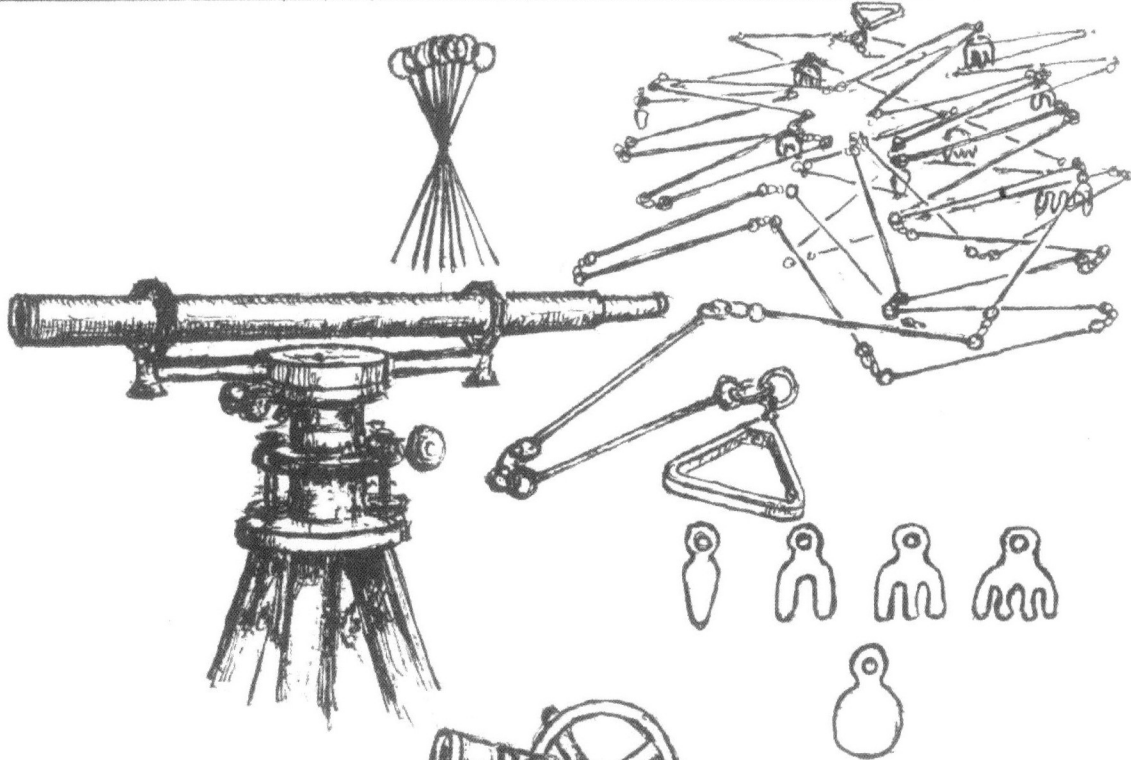

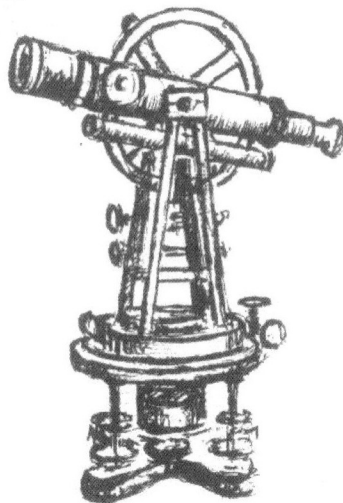

Surveying the route was carried out by triangulation as illustrated *right*. A measured distance was established on the ground and used as a base line. The angles from this base to a distant object were then measured. With this information, and using the knowledge of the ratios of the sides of a right angled triangle, the distances between observed points could then be calculated. Scaled down, these measurements were then plotted onto a map - triangle being added to triangle until the whole area had thus been covered. The route of the canal's planned course - together with details of streams, roads and estate boundaries, would then be filled in - all this data being needed for the Act of Incorporation required before the waterway could be built.

By the mid eighteenth century surveying instruments had been perfected sufficiently for such work to be done. Typical instruments are shown on the opposite page. Distance measuring along the ground was achieved by the Gunter chain, of late sixteenth century origin. It might be from two to four poles long: a pole is approximately 5 metres (5.5 yards). The arrows were planted as the chain progressed. The level *middle opposite* with its telescope and spirit level was developed in the seventeenth century, while the theodolite *bottom opposite* which could measure both horizontal and vertical angles dated from

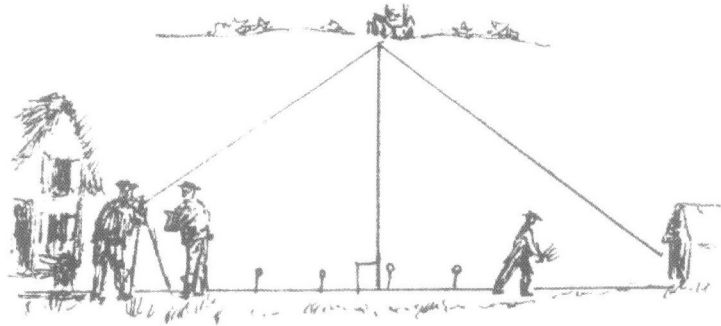

1720. It was used in making the observations for triangulation.

With the route worked out by triangulation, details of the cutting needed were secured by levelling. This determined height differences, or as the cutter would see it, depth differences. The levelling instrument would be used to sight adjustable markers on staffs held in front and behind. The surveyor would signal to the staff-holders to move their markers until they lined up in the telescope. The differences in height of the markers gave the height of one staff position relative to the other, and so by arithmetic the depth that needed to be dug in order to achieve a level line, would be established. That level line was the top of the canal bank.

When the course of the canal had been established, work could begin on the ground. The first task was to mark out the route by driving level pegs every 40 to 60 metres along the line of the bank. Their crosspieces were aligned using levelling instruments; for the depth to be dug would be known from the previous survey of levels. Whatever the height of the crosspiece above the ground, that would be the depth required to be dug. At earthworks they were sited closer. Opposite them, pegs were set out to mark the centre of the canal line, "staking the middle range".

Next came a series of holes, "slope holes", at each side. Like the level pegs, they were dug every 40 to 60 metres. These holes indicated the course and width of the water channel. They were joined up by trenches on either bank called "lock spits" - which made the course of the canal clear. A spade's depth, the lock spit was dug with care, with the spade entering the turf at the angle of slope decided for the bank. 1:1.5 was usual. A workman threw out the wedge of turf. The illustration *above* shows all of this.

Early canals tended to avoid heavy earthworks, partly to save expense, partly because of construction difficulties. A height contour was chosen and the canal followed it, terraced out of the hillside and avoiding locks.

James Brindley and his followers were the arch advocates of the contour canal which, they argued, would serve more places by winding about. Nowhere is this more apparent than on the Oxford Canal *below left* where Wormleighton Hill is encircled by a loop which almost comes back on itself.

Over half a century later, canal engineers were more confident. Not only did they straighten tortuous lines, as on this same Oxford's northern section, but drove new lines direct across country, as Telford's route for the main line of the Birmingham and Liverpool Junction, (now the Shropshire Union) so clearly demonstrates. This involved massive earthworks such as the Shelmore embankment *below right*.

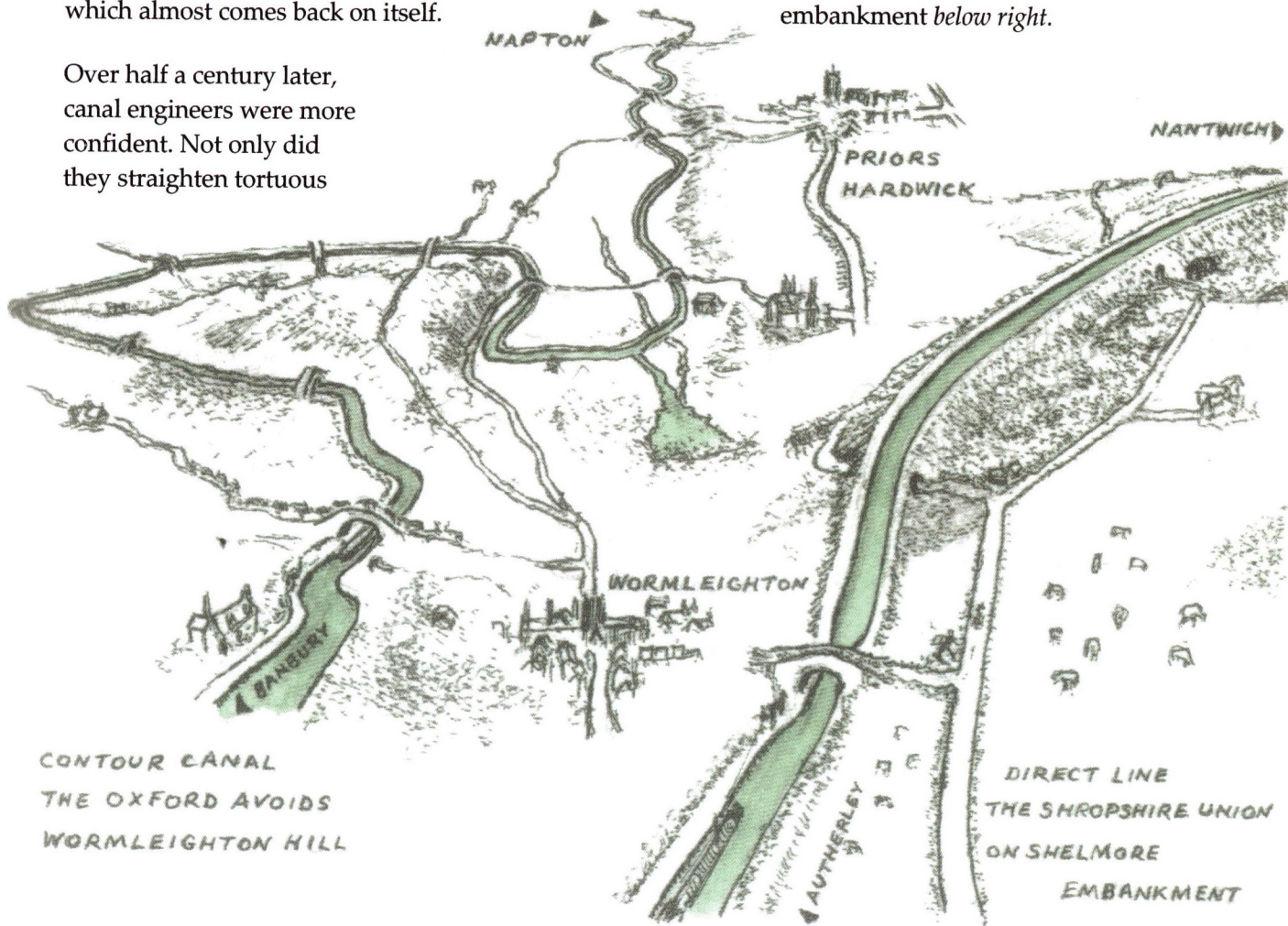

NAPTON

PRIORS HARDWICK

NANTWICH

WORMLEIGHTON

BANBURY

CONTOUR CANAL
THE OXFORD AVOIDS
WORMLEIGHTON HILL

AUTHERLEY

DIRECT LINE
THE SHROPSHIRE UNION
ON SHELMORE
EMBANKMENT

DIGGING AND PUDDLING

Cutting depended on muscle power for the whole period of river improvement and canal building, except at the end of the nineteenth century when steam excavators tackled the Manchester Ship Canal. Tools were simple; pick, spade and wheelbarrow. A narrow spade was used to work clay puddle into a plastic state for applying to sides and bottom of the canal to make it watertight, and a "scope" was needed to dribble water onto the puddle while it was being worked. The blocks, *below right* called "horsing blocks", supported planks for wheeling the barrows when carrying away the spoil.

Shallow sided wheelbarrows carried 100 kg (220 lbs) of spoil or "stuff", while bricks and stone were moved on barrows without sides, but with a head-board against which materials could be stacked. Blocks of stone were handled on two wheeled trolleys.

LEVEL CUTTING

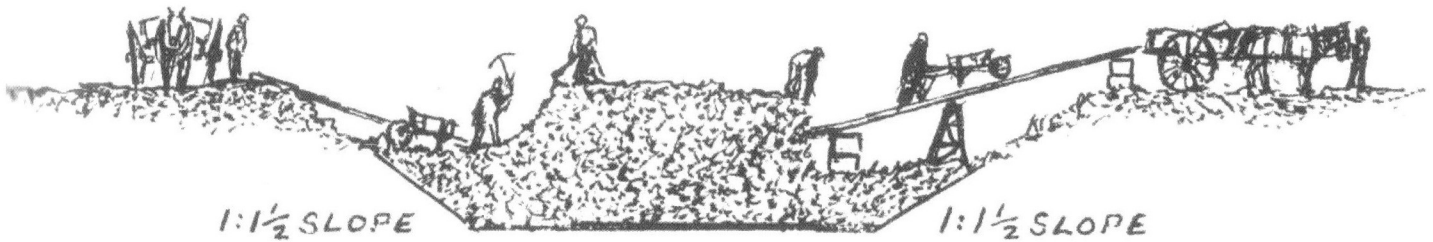

1:1½ SLOPE   1:1½ SLOPE

The illustrations here show the sequence of cutting; level cutting *above* and terracing *below*. In both cases the men worked inward from the lock spits, "reaching" back by vertical cuts and wheeling away the spoil. When terracing, they would work back from the lower lock spit first, building up the lower bank as they progressed. Sods were used to consolidate the banks and, because of puddling needs, the canal was dug deeper and wider than the eventual cross section. Another method of cutting was that of "benching", whereby the men at the bottom threw spoil up to barrows on stagings half way up the sides parallel with the canal. Men on the stagings worked on the upper parts of the bank. Benching is illustrated in the *frontispiece* to this book.

TERRACING

ORIGINAL GROUND

BUILT UP BANK   1:1½ SLOPE   1:1½ SLOPE

Spoil removal was the most expensive part of canal cutting. It was either dumped nearby by tip cart or carried away for use elsewhere on the line, often to create an embankment on the "cut and fill" principle *above*.

Stone blocks for the bank coping, for lock chamber sides and bridge abutments arrived by two horse flat waggons *below*. Without cranes the blocks had to be shifted by lever and rollers and skidded down planks before being hand hauled into position.

To hold water in porous ground, the canal had to be lined with "puddle". Clay or heavy loam mixed with water takes up so much moisture, but after a while can absorb no more and becomes a sealant.

Puddle was prepared by chopping clay with a narrow spade and watering with a scope. It was then applied in layers, keyed into each other with the spade. The layers at the sides were each some 25 cms (9-10 inches) thick, protected by a top dressing of earth or sods. These came up to the surface of the water, indeed to the bank edge. The lining across the bottom was nearly a metre (3 feet) thick, likewise built up in layers. Extra protection could be given by a puddle ditch or puddle gutter when the canal was embanked *above*, a metre wide and as deep as necessary. Puddle ditches had the added asset of deterring water rats and moles and could be reinforced by piling. It has been said that cattle *below* were driven down new canal beds to consolidate the puddle before water was let in; certainly their cloven hooves would have had a binding effect. Normally the workmen would work and tamp the puddle into the canal bed as it was applied.

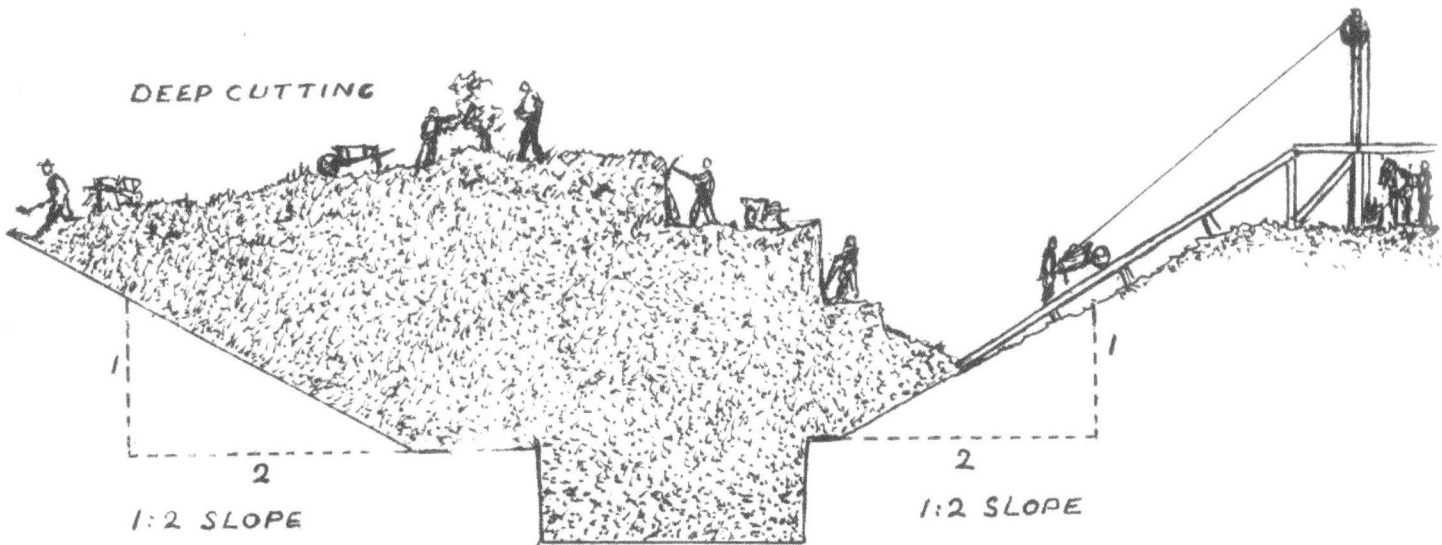

DEEP CUTTING

1:2 SLOPE

1:2 SLOPE

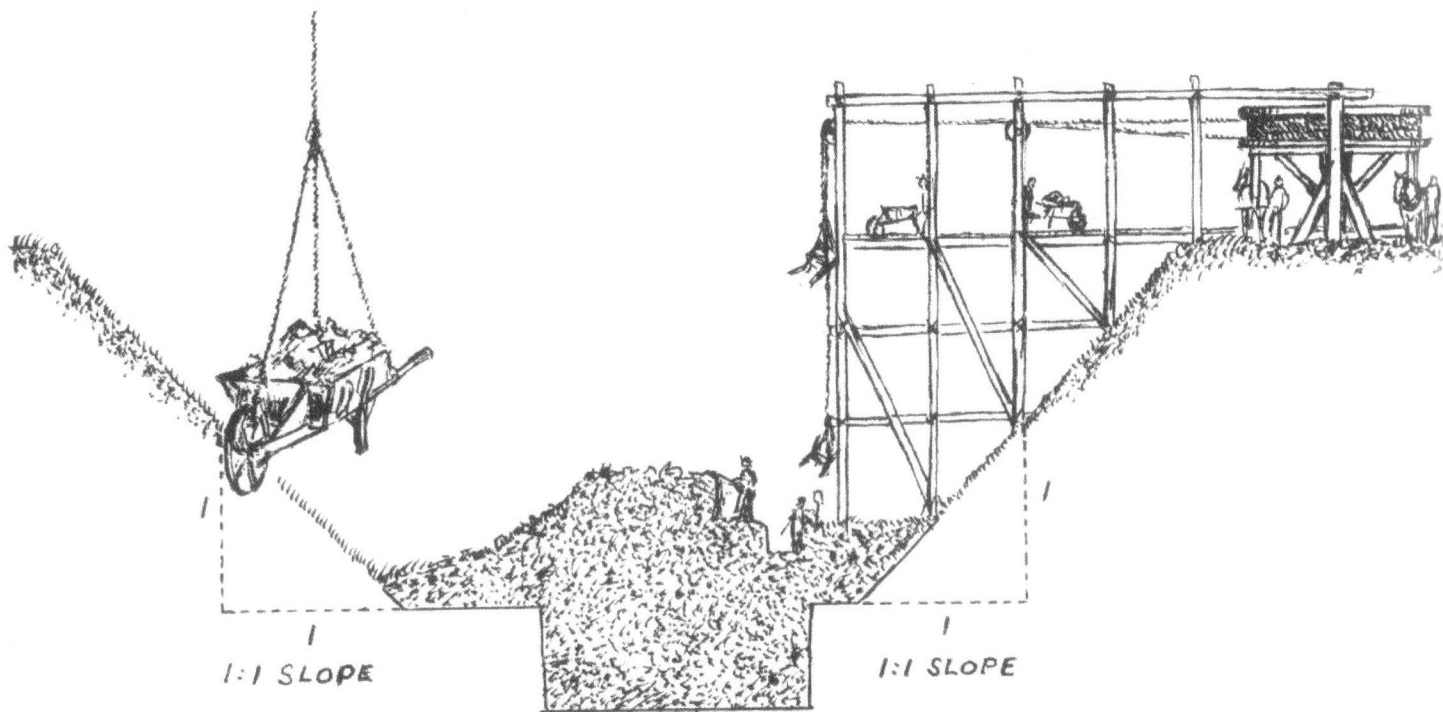

1:1 SLOPE

1:1 SLOPE

Deep cutting and embanking demanded greater concentration of labour, while deep cutting created extra problems in spoil removal as illustrated *opposite*. A 25° slope, general for canal embanking, was equally desirable for deep cutting but not always used. For example on the Shropshire Union Canal, a steep 50° slope in a cutting ninety feet deep was chosen, which has led to many slips.

Spoil was removed by horse worked "gins" or "whims", lifting out barrows by a three tailed whip. Almost all the patent digging machines of the canal building period were in fact spoil removal machines. An early one was John Carne's, employed on the Herefordshire and Gloucestershire Canal in 1793. This used a horse whim to lift buckets; eight men filling them. In the nineteenth century, barrow runs were used, often horse worked, following railway practice.

Embankments demanded spoil, at first taken from alongside the work, but later brought up by cart or even by boat from deep cuttings elsewhere - the "cut and fill" technique shown *below*. Banking in some form or another was generally needed for every mile of canal dug. Sometimes this would be a free standing embankment pushing across open country - but more often would be the bank supporting the outside of the canal cut across sloping ground. Spoil was taken from the cut made into the slope. A 25° angle of embanking on either side was best - and because the banks were built up, they were usually reinforced by a puddle ditch.

CUT AND FILL

LINE OF CANAL BANK

TIPPING

SIDE CUTTING

PROTECTING THE BANKS

Once built, the waterways then needed to be protected against the damage that the passage of boats can so easily create. Bank protection was as necessary to the canals as to the rivers in spite of their lack of current. The arrival of powered craft increased this need.

A simple precaution was a ledge or "berm" *top left opposite* just below the surface. In this, rushes could be planted to bind the sides and break eroding waves. The ledge itself would have a similar effect and also helped stop debris rolling into the canal.

Banks could be stiffened by camp shedding (called "boarding and slabbing" on the Leeds and Liverpool) or by the more primitive use of stakes holding back brushwood *top right opposite*.

Stone pitching *centre opposite* was applied to canals as well as rivers, notably on the Bridgewater when the steam tugs were introduced in the 1870s, and it was essential on the Manchester Ship Canal to resist the suction created by the passage of 10,000 gross ton ships.

Sheet piling in unbroken lengths *bottom right opposite* is the most effective for checking leaks. In the eighteenth century it was made up of grooved piles driven close up, with lengths of deal slipped down the grooves to make the seal. Concrete piles were introduced between the two world wars, and in the 1950s their use was increased to overcome the backlog of bank maintenance. They proved heavy and awkward. Waling (horizontal strengthening) often from light railway line was used to tie them together and every fifth pile was anchored back.

Today interlocked steel sheet piling is favoured, held by crash barrier waling and anchored at every third pile.

Pile driving *bottom left opposite* has been by maul, by vertically falling weight and by compressed air hammer. Essential to accuracy is the jig to ensure alignment, with two planks being spaced to the thickness of the pile. Infilling may later be made using spoil from dredging. This is usually applied in three stages to allow for drying out, settlement and consolidation.

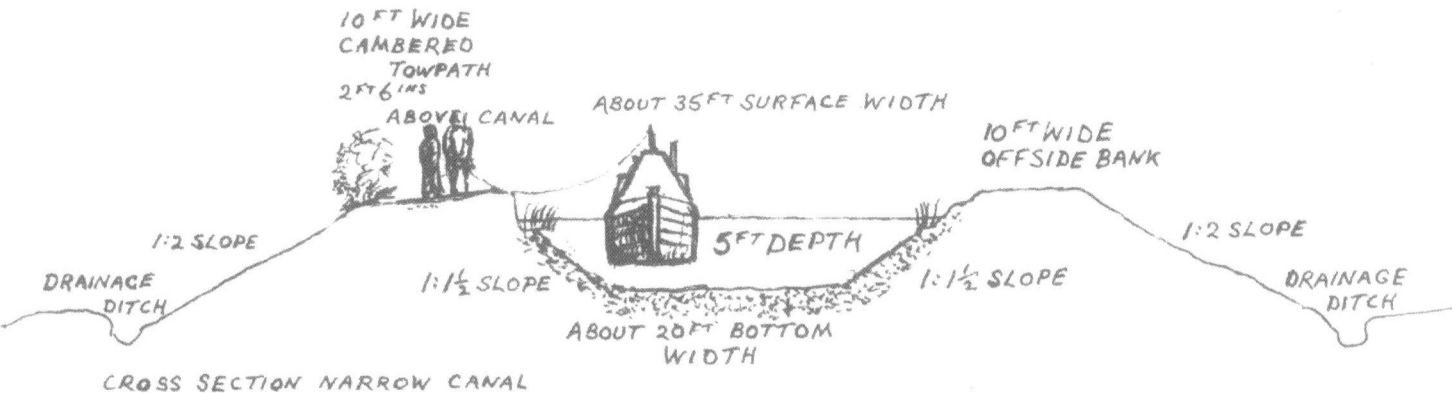

10 FT WIDE
CAMBERED
TOWPATH
2 FT 6 INS
ABOVE CANAL

ABOUT 35 FT SURFACE WIDTH

10 FT WIDE
OFFSIDE BANK

1:2 SLOPE

DRAINAGE
DITCH

1:1½ SLOPE

5 FT DEPTH

1:1½ SLOPE

1:2 SLOPE

DRAINAGE
DITCH

ABOUT 20 FT BOTTOM
WIDTH

CROSS SECTION NARROW CANAL

It is worth comparing the dimensions of the two main canal variants. A narrow canal *above,* such as most of those in the Midlands, was designed to be some 11 or 12 metres wide across the surface with a bottom width of 6 metres and a 1.5 to 2 metre depth. The canal sides would slope at an angle of 1:1.5 and the outer bank at 1:2, a standard gradient throughout. A broad canal like the Leeds and Liverpool *below* would have a surface width of 15 metres and a bed some 10 metres across, with a depth comparable to a narrow canal, but frequently deeper.

Eventually a formula was worked out for the best cross sectional area, allowing boats to pass with ease at a reasonable speed, dependent on the ability of water to flow back past the hull. The least breadth of bottom should be twice the maximum beam of boats usually using the canal, and the least depth should be the greatest draught of a boat plus 25cms, and the least cross sectional area six times the area of the boat's midship section.

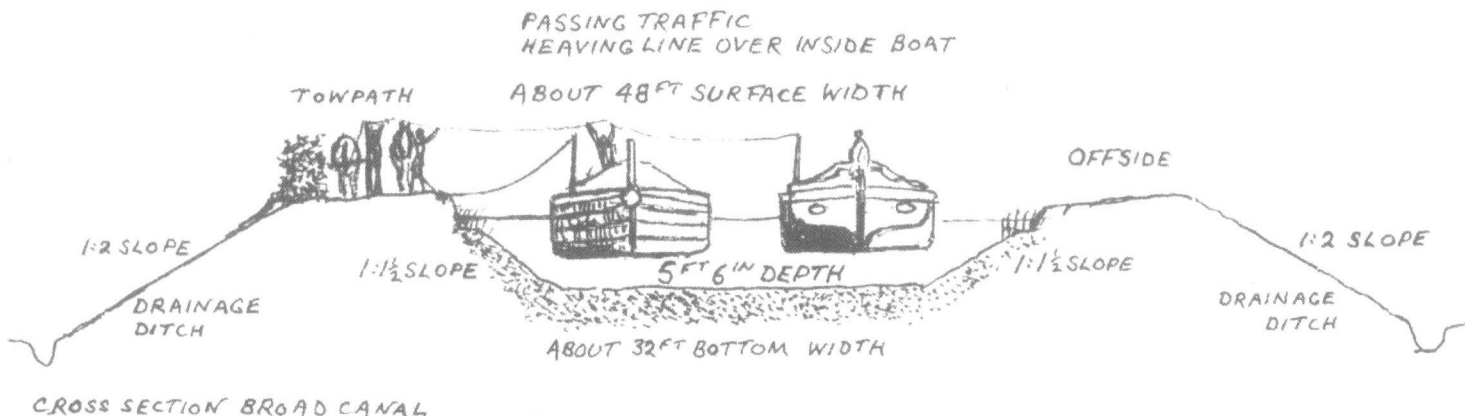

PASSING TRAFFIC
HEAVING LINE OVER INSIDE BOAT

ABOUT 48 FT SURFACE WIDTH

TOWPATH

OFFSIDE

1:2 SLOPE

DRAINAGE
DITCH

1:1½ SLOPE

5 FT 6 IN DEPTH

1:1½ SLOPE

1:2 SLOPE

DRAINAGE
DITCH

ABOUT 32 FT BOTTOM WIDTH

CROSS SECTION BROAD CANAL

The Leeds and Liverpool illustration *opposite* shows the difficulty of boats and horses meeting and passing; lines were being either dropped or passed over one another. Canal bylaws stipulated who was to give way; a highway code of some complexity.

Embankments had to be pierced by culverts to take streams, cattle creeps and even roads. The great banks on the Shropshire Union, Shebdon and Shelmore *upper left*, are burrowed under by minor roads. The Grand Junction's embankments at

Wolverton, *upper right,* flanking the aqueduct, have two cattle creeps beneath them, while at Catterall, *lower right,* the River Calder is culverted under the Lancaster Canal.

ACROSS THE VALLEY AND UNDER THE HILL

Canal engineers had to face up to the need for aqueducts from an early stage, although they were not much liked. A flight of locks and a level crossing was considered much safer, and such was the initial temporary line that the Grand Junction Canal took to cross the River Ouse at Wolverton. Europe and the Romans had led the way with aqueducts. There was one near Milan in the fifteenth century and when the Canal du Midi opened in 1681, it crossed the Valley of the Repudre by a major structure; the world's first boat carrying aqueduct. The New River Company built several aqueducts for its water supply channel from Ware to London which opened in 1613, but the first boat aqueduct in Britain was John Gilbert's and James Brindley's striking structure over the Irwell, built to take the Duke's Canal from Worsley into Manchester *top opposite*. Opened in 1761 it crossed the navigation at Barton by three arches bearing the canal nearly 12 metres above the river in a 6 metre wide trough. This was heavily puddled and thus of a great weight; a feature which posed problems in future aqueduct designs. Single line working was the rule over the Barton aqueduct, controlled in later years by semaphore signals. The central arch had to be high and wide enough to clear the masts of sailing flats on the Irwell, and to resist the weight and lateral pressure of the canal and its approach embankment, each face wall was given an inwards lean (or "batter") aided by substantial buttressing of walls and abutments. All the basic engineering problems of building aqueducts were demonstrated and successfully solved at Barton.

Most commonly, aqueducts are built to take canals over river valleys. More rarely do aqueducts carry canal over canal. The illustration *centre opposite* shows that at Denford near Leek. It was completed in 1841 to carry the Leek branch of the Caldon over the Caldon itself. This had to be because of railway building, which demanded the resiting of the canal's junction away from the permanent way.

The third illustration *bottom opposite* brings the subject back to Barton, but this time over the Manchester Ship Canal. When built, the Ship Canal swallowed up the Mersey and Irwell Navigation, but the line of the Bridgewater Canal had to be kept. The solution was a structure unique in the world; the swinging aqueduct at Barton was opened in 1893.

Designed by Sir Edward Leader Williams, the engineer of the Ship Canal, it has a span of 72 metres and contains water weighing 1473 tons. It is swung by electric power. Rams work the sealing doors of both tank and canal and force home rubber seals when the tank is united with the Bridgewater. Down from the aqueduct is the Barton swing road bridge, and further down again is the high level bridge of the motorway. In the illustration one of the paddle tugs that predated the motorway is seen.

The building of an aqueduct is best illustrated in stages. Shown here is that of the Vyrnwy aqueduct in North Wales, which takes the Montgomeryshire Canal over the river near the junction of its Eastern Branch with the Ellesmere Canal at Carreghofa.

It was completed by 1797, built of stone with five arches, three over the river and two over the land. Construction did not go smoothly for one arch collapsed. By 1823, all five arches were found to be fractured and in need of reinforcement. This was carried out with tie rods to prevent the outward collapse of the face walls. Two arches needed still further reinforcement with straps to keep their shape and, like the tie rods, these are visible today.

The illustration shows the sequence of building; the various stages obviously being completed at different times. To the left, men are digging the foundations for the piers and abutments of the land based arches. There is a cofferdam round the river pier under construction to prevent water entering the workings. Building the piers and buttresses was necessary before arches could be

started, as they had to spring from substantial abutments. Centring had then to be inserted to support the masonry.

With the arches finished, the stone face walls could be built up and the whole then filled with rubble up to the level of the canal bed which was then laid and puddled. The towpath was added, commonly built out over the canal bed to allow a greater cross sectional area of water; otherwise a laden boat in a seven foot wide channel would be pushing a wall of water ahead of herself.

A simple crane would have been used to handle the masonry, while wheeling planks for supporting the barrows being pushed across the muddy site, would be much in evidence. Many materials would have come by boat from the Ellesmere Canal.

Materials for aqueducts can range from brick and stone to iron and concrete; the choice of materials influencing design. Brindley, when left to himself, chose to build aqueducts far less spectacular than Barton. A section of one of these *top right* is representative of his approach. He would cross a river at as low a level as possible, using many shallow arches to support the great weight of his heavy puddle lined troughs. His twenty three arched aqueduct, built in brick over the River Dove, has side walls nearly 4 metres thick, each made up of two 45cms brick walls, with clay puddle between them. The water channel for the Trent and Mersey is 9 metres wide, so the whole structure is no less than 16 metres wide from face wall to face wall. The arches, more like tunnel portals in appearance, are of 4.5 metres span.

Many of the South Wales aqueducts and yet more in the Midlands are in the Brindley tradition. That at Vyrnwy can be included among them. But other engineers became more venturesome. John Rennie was one of these, and the masonry aqueduct at Dundas *bottom left* which carries the Kennet and Avon Canal over the River Avon near Bath is a monument to his mastery of classical design. It has a 20 metres (66 feet) span central arch with two parabolic arches to take flood water.

Avoncliff aqueduct nearby is less pretentious, but the greatest Rennie achievement must be the Lune aqueduct at Lancaster with   five stone arches reinforced by internal inverted arches and, as at Dundas, by lateral tie rods whose ends are concealed in masonry. Whereas Rennie put great weight on his arches, Benjamin Outram on the Peak Forest went in the other direction, cutting holes in the spandrels of the three arches of his Marple aqueduct in order to lessen the weight.

Much controversy surrounds the introduction of cast iron to aqueduct building. Who thought of it first? Cast iron had the advantage of doing away with the heavy puddle lining and seemed likely to resist lateral water pressure with success. The first cast iron aqueduct at The Holmes on the Derby Canal was completed in February 1796. A modest 13.5 metres (44 feet 6 inches) long iron trough, it was soon eclipsed by the Shrewsbury Canal's aqueduct at Longdon-on-Tern *upper illustration* of March 1796 built to replace a collapsed and un-completed aqueduct of masonry. Longdon at 19 metres (62 yards) long is not exciting to look, at but at least it did prove the capabilities of cast iron. (Only two of its three piers are illustrated here.)

The next development was far and away more ambitious; to build two aqueducts for the Ellesmere Canal to cross the River Ceiriog and Dee at Chirk and Pontcysyllte. The decision to do so was taken before Longdon was completed. Chirk opened in 1801, a masonry aqueduct concealing an iron trough - as if to show the engineers were not entirely confident in the new material. Pontcysyllte followed in 1805. An iron trough was carried on nineteen cast iron arches of 14 metres (45 feet) span, resting on masonry piers 38 metres (126 feet) above the Dee. The towpath was built out over the trough, the whole structure being 307 metres (1,007 feet) long. The arches were made up of four cast iron members; the inner two openwork, the outer pair solid under a trough constructed of flanged and bolted plates. William Jessop seems to have been the main instigator of these two aqueducts. He had experienced trouble with masonry aqueducts on the Cromford Canal and was to have more when his brick aqueduct over the River Ouse at Wolverton collapsed in 1808. Cast iron must have offered an attractive alternative. The Ouse aqueduct was replaced by one of cast iron *lower illustration* on brick piers. Designed by Benjamin Bevan, it was opened in 1811. Again flanged bolted plates were used to build the trough.

No illustration of the building of a cast iron aqueduct has survived, but it can be assumed that prefabrication methods were employed. On Pontcysyllte, the four arched members must each have been delivered complete to the site from William Hazeldine's nearby ironworks at Plas Kynaston, and then secured to the piers. The trough sections would have Followed, and been bolted through as the illustration *right* shows; bottoms first, and then the segmental sides.

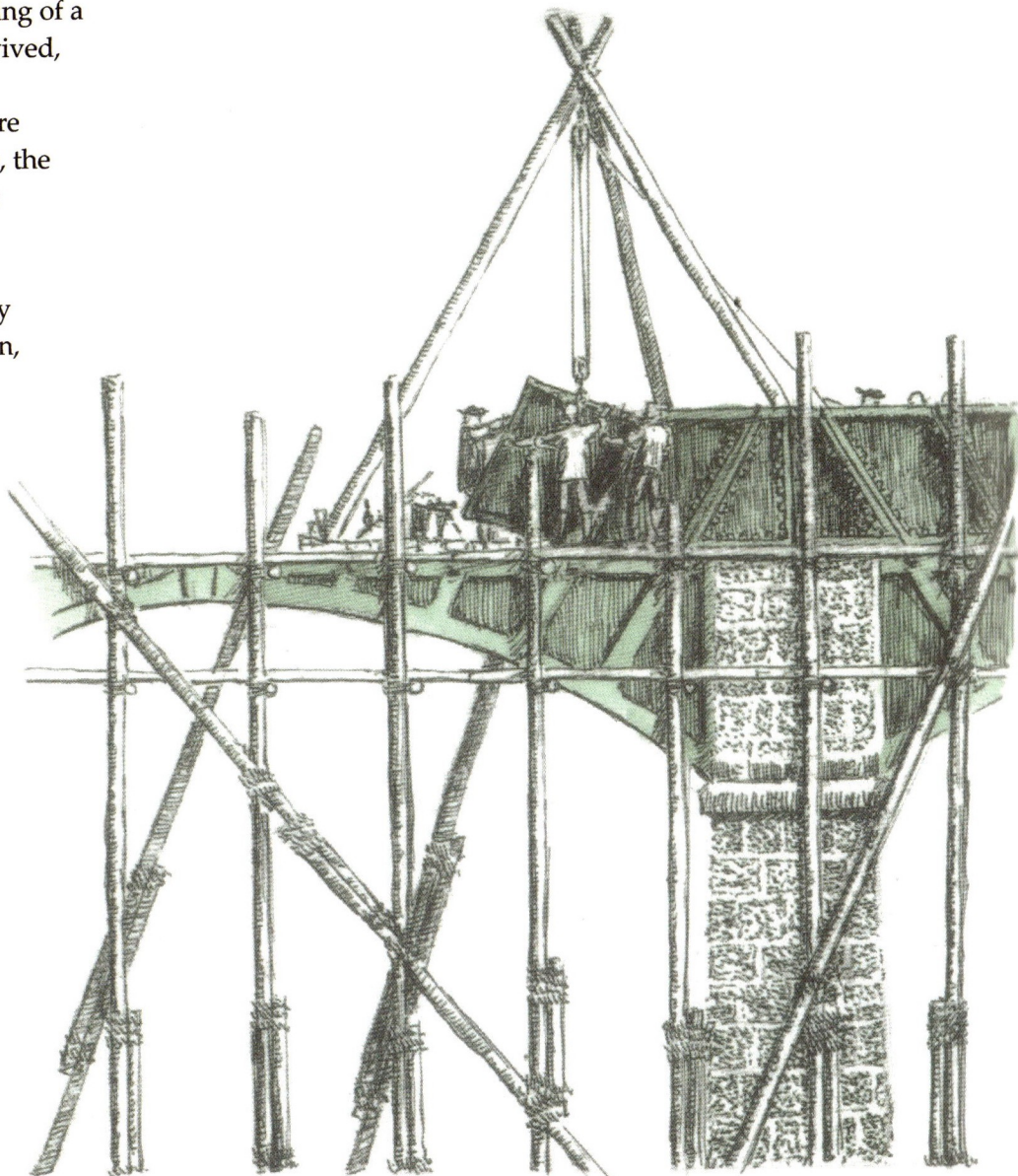

Strangely little attention has been paid to the strikingly different style of aqueduct over the Calder at Stanley Ferry, *above*, opened in 1839 which carries the Wakefield line of the Aire and Calder Navigation. It is unlike any other aqueduct in this country, for it is dependent on an overall arch to carry the trough beneath it. The arch span is 55 metres (180 feet) and both it and the trough are built up of cast iron plates with wrought iron supporting rods. The cast iron embellishment used at Stanley Ferry would have delighted John Rennie; cast iron Doric columns along the trough sides and classical pediments at each end. The engineer was George Leather the younger, modernizer of the Aire and Calder and creator of the inland port of Goole; a man who deserves to be remembered. Since 1981 a single span concrete trough has lain alongside it to carry barge traffic, but the older aqueduct still remains navigable.

Road and railway spanning aqueducts are many; cast iron on the Shropshire Union, stone on the Lancaster, brick on the Basingstoke. The railway aqueducts have been altered when tracks have been quadrupled and electrification undertaken - while motorways have also made changes to the canal scene. The Tame Valley Canal crosses a slip road to the M5 at Stone Cross near West Bromwich and the Leeds and Liverpool crosses the M65 near Blackburn. Concrete is the principal material for these modern canal carrying structures.

Aqueducts might be expensive, but tunnels were more so; troublesome to build, canal engineers liked to avoid them if possible.

TUNNELS

Tunnels were generally the first works to be started and the last to be finished, often by a long margin. This could delay opening so much that a tramroad might have to be laid along their top to carry traffic prior to completion, as was needed at Blisworth on the Grand Junction. A tunnel at a summit was often inevitable, but they were also needed lower down where deep cuttings and terracing proved unstable. This happened on the Trent and Mersey Canal, which makes use of two such tunnels at Barnton and Saltersford. In contrast a tunnel might be planned, but the rock then found too unstable to bore, as was the case at Gnosall on the Shropshire Union. Here, what was to be a longish tunnel ended up as a short one plus a long cutting.

Making a tunnel started with the alignment of a cord on the surface, the line being marked out by pegs. Then followed the selection of shaft sites. The more shafts there were the better - as work could proceed outwards in each direction from their bottoms, as well as inwards from the portals. By surveying on the surface and establishing height differences, it was possible to work out the depth of each shaft, so that all descended to a common level. The illustrations *opposite* show the stages: setting out the line *top,* and levelling to establish shaft depth, *upper right;* shaft sinking *centre* which

involved winding out the spoil with a horse whim *below* on which so much depended in the days of canal building. These machines, examples of which were at work in small collieries even into the 1940s, generally depended on two blinkered horses turning a drum, some 7 metres (24 feet) in diameter, from which one rope wound up as the other descended. The buckets would contain about 200 - 250 kg (4-5 cwt) of spoil each. Shaft sinking is an old art, derived from sinking wells. As the diggers went down, a ring or "curb" went down too - and on this the lining was set, the bricks or stone being added course by course as the level dropped.

46

Tunnel boring is best portrayed in stages. In reality all the shafts would be sunk before any tunnelling started and a pilot tunnel would be completed - before enlarging this to full bore and lining. With the shafts aligned on the surface, the next task was to align what would become the headings at the foot of each shaft. This was done by dropping two plumb lines down each shaft, all aligned on the surface by using the level and markers. When correctly aligned, a cord linking them would indicate the direction of the headings. A still day was needed for this delicate operation. The

accuracy of most canal tunnels is impressive; only two short ones, Barnton and Saltersford (mentioned on page 46) are noticeably kinked. It was the practice to sink as many shafts as possible, and close most of them up afterwards, leaving just a few for ventilation. However, when steam tunnel tugs were introduced some shafts had to be opened up again.

Tunnelling without geological knowledge was a chancy business, and water and quicksands were often encountered. The water could either be

pumped out or drained away by a sough; a drift mine practice. Ventilation was achieved by lighting fires at one shaft bottom to draw air down a neighbouring shaft, while illumination was by candle. Blasting loosened the earth and rock, the shotholes being bored by hand auger while iron stemmers rammed home the loose black powder, in spite of the danger from sparks. Copper would have been safer. Spoil was wound up by the horse whim or gin and sometimes a tramroad would be built from the headings to the shaft bottom. Enlarging the pilot tunnel to finished bore size

required staging and centring for the brick or stone work, which was also laid across the bottom to stiffen the sides and seal the canal bed.

The cross section of Blisworth *top right* shows the shape of one of the country's major canal tunnels, 2794 metres (3056 yards) long, on the main line of the Grand Junction. The brickwork here is 43cms (17 inches) thick round the sides and roof and 33 cms (13 inches) thick round the invert.

Because they were privately financed, canal tunnels were usually as small and plain as possible. The first tunnel at Harecastle on the Trent and Mersey was completed in 1775 and had the tightest of dimensions; one narrow boat's width and no towing path. Since it took two or three hours to leg through - lying on the foredeck or cabin top and pushing with the feet - traffic delays were considerable. Telford's second Harecastle tunnel, completed in 1827, was also only a single boat's width, but it did have a towing path, although many horses would be loath to use it. Fortunately the tunnels of the Grand Junction, Blisworth and Braunston, were built to broad standard, and would allow narrow boats past each other.

Looking at the portal illustrations opposite, the *top left* shows the natural cavern of Armitage on the Trent and Mersey, now opened out. Like many short tunnels, it had a towpath.

Stanedge *top right* is Britain's longest canal tunnel at just over 4988 metres (5456 yards) and burrows 183 metres (600 feet) under the Pennines. It took seventeen years to build and was opened in 1811 to a single narrow boat width, but was provided with four passing places. The sides and roof were mostly left unlined.

Sapperton, *upper centre* 3490 metres (3817 yards) on the Thames and Severn, opened in 1789, has perhaps the most ornate portals of any. Shown here is the south eastern or Coates end in classical style while that at Daneway at the head of the Golden Valley *lower left* is more severe. The Coates portal is now restored but Daneway needs attention after decades of vandalism.

Last of the canal tunnels to be built was Netherton *lower right* 2768 metres (3027 yards) long on the Birmingham system. Built well within the railway age, it was finished in 1858, to a generous size, two boats' widths and with two towpaths. Netherton was originally lit by gas, and later by electricity. Note, by the way, the guard rails for the horses.

Finally *bottom centre* is an early tunnel; Preston Brook. At 1133 metres (1239 yards) this takes the Trent and Mersey to join the Bridgewater. It was intended to be wide enough for broad craft such as Mersey flats, but was never used by them. From 1854, tugs were in use at Preston Brook as well as at Barnton and Saltersford, for none had towpaths. Two of the tugs were fitted with guide wheels at their sides to keep them on course.

CHANGING THE LEVEL

Locks, or to be specific pound locks, are what people tend to think of first when a canal is mentioned. They are the key to the canal's mastery of hills and valleys. Pound locks date back to the tenth century in China and the fourteenth century in Europe. The illustrations *below* show how a boat climbs up and down hill; up on the *left*, down on the *right*. Illustrated are narrow locks, approx 2 metres x 20 metres (7 feet wide x 70 feet), as found say on the Staffordshire and Worcestershire Canal and indeed throughout the Midlands. The boat enters with the bottom gates open and the top one closed. Once the boat is in, the gates are closed and the paddles or sluices of the lower gates are closed too. The upper or top paddles are drawn, first those by the side of the lock, (the ground paddles) then the gate paddle. These allow the lock to fill with water. When the boat has risen to the top of the lock, and the water levels within it and the upper section (or pound) of the canal are equal, the paddles are closed and the top gate is opened to allow the boat to pass out of the lock, and on its journey.

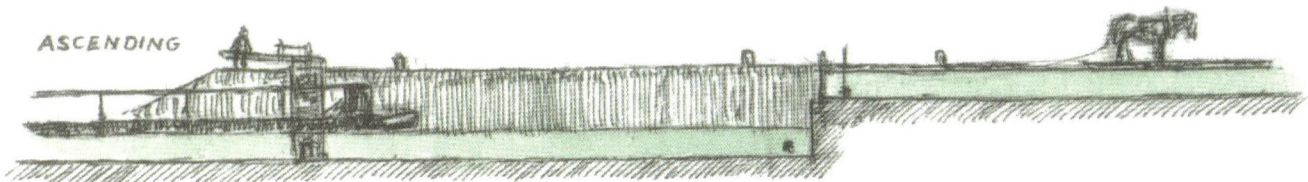

ASCENDING

Descending requires the reverse. The bottom gates are shut and the lock is filled with water. This allows the top gate to be opened. When closed behind the boat, the top paddles are dropped (i.e. closed) too. The bottom paddles (generally found on the gates) are opened (drawn) and the boat sinks to the level of the lower pound. When this has happened, the bottom gates are opened and the boat leaves. All this presupposes the lock is set for the boat, i.e. empty for going uphill and full for going down; but often the lock ahead is found full when the boat is ascending and vice versa. Filling and emptying takes time; hence in cargo carrying days the need for a "lock wheeler" on a cycle to go ahead and prepare the locks. Disputes could arise if boats were approaching the lock from opposite directions. The Grand Junction put up posts; first past the post won the lock, but stealing a march on the other boat was part of canal life.

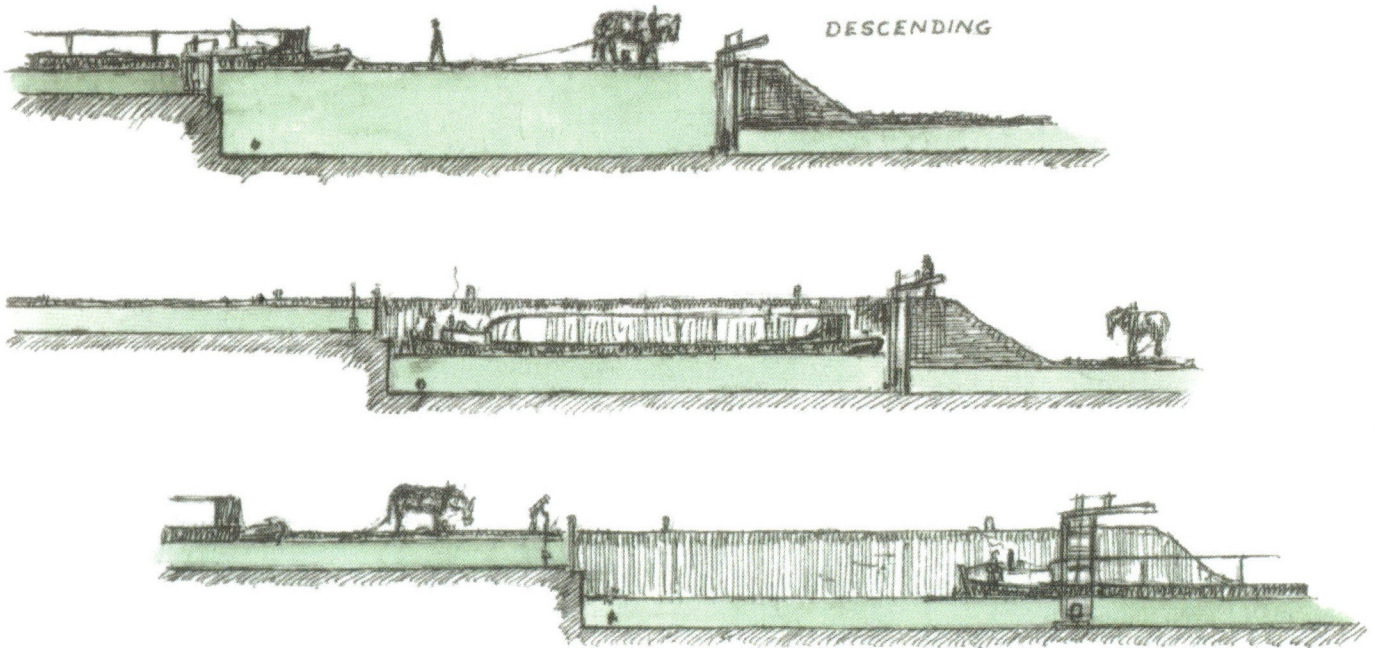

DESCENDING

Where a rapid change of level had to be overcome, locks were grouped with top and bottom gates common to both; a "riser" or "staircase" of two, three, four or even five locks. Whereas a two rise lock is not too extravagant, anything bigger would require the drawing down of several lockfuls of water to lift an ascending boat.

The five rise at Bingley *above* on the Leeds and Liverpool Canal is the largest group in an area full of staircases. The locks below such "risers" were ensured an adequate supply of water - but for those locks and pounds above, water supply was an ever recurrent problem.

The three diagrams *opposite* illustrate three different approaches to locking. The single locks at the top are separated at slightly different levels, though in reality they would be wide apart; while the locks in the *centre* flight are much closer together. Normally a couple of boats' lengths would separate locks to provide the minimum reservoir of water needed for the lock below. If locks are built very close together, the intermediate pounds have to be extended sideways. This was done at Runcorn on the flight down to the docks, and at Devizes on the flight of twenty nine locks down Caen Hill. One notable flight - at The Bratch on the Staffordshire and Worcestershire - has its three locks grouped so closely that they must be treated as a staircase, as no boats can lie in the pounds between. Finally, a three rise staircase is illustrated *below,* with two boats going up. This shows how lockfuls of water have to be drawn off in order to make a staircase work

Where traffic was heavy, pairs of locks built in parallel were used on some canals to allow boats to pass more easily. Paired locks had other advantages. Boats in pairs could lock up and down together, and the second lock could be used as a reservoir (rather like a side pond) when linked to its neighbour by an interconnecting paddle. The Cheshire locks of the Trent and Mersey *below* provide an example of paired locks. A regular practice was for boats to lock down "with six paddles up". Using the two interconnecting paddles plus four on the two sets of bottom gates this provided a quick way of emptying a lock and speeding up the journey.

Lock construction started by selecting the position for the upper sill, for this would determine the rise. The whole area then had to be dug out. A pit, extra big if it was to be a staircase, was excavated. The chambers had to be built free standing to ensure stability, hence a large pit. Good foundations were needed for the side walls and this meant using piling, not only down the sides hut also under the sills at each end. Another need was for a strong breast wall at the head of the lock to contain the upper pound. The lock bottom was generally a brick or stone invert which gave added strength to the sides. These sides were made extra secure by an outwards batter (i.e. slope) and they were also buttressed along their length outside the chamber in order to resist water pressure. The buttresses were tied into the side walls by H shaped oak brackets, while the sills of oak spiked to elm were supported by layers of elm and deal flooring. To check leakage of water from the surrounding ground, puddle was applied between the buttresses. The illustration *lower opposite* shows all these features. Much of lock construction is hidden from view - including the culverts *upper illustration* which carry the water from the top ground paddles into the chamber.

Another sequence view *above*, this time of lock construction, to illustrate what has already been described.

Choosing the place for the upper sill and working out the rise demanded levelling. It was an advantage if locks had equal rises, for gates could be made to standard dimensions, an ideal which was achieved on the Rochdale Canal. The pit was dug out and the chamber built on the piled foundations needed for the walls and sills. Scaffolding was used when building up the side walls and much work went on by the side of the lock. A kiln for brick production and a saw pit for preparing timber for the sills and floorings would be in use. A procession of horses and carts with materials would arrive; coal for the kiln, lime for mortar, timber, scaffolding poles, ladders, planking, and the pile driving rig, all on their way. Lock gates and piling would usually be made in the canal's central workshops and would be delivered by boat if the canal was in water up to the site. If not it would be a matter of yet more horse transport.

Lock gates are held in their quoins by water pressure but swing true by means of a pin at the foot of the heel post with a collar round this same post at the top. A single gate closes against a stout facing in the opposite wall, but double gates are mitred and forced together by water pressure.

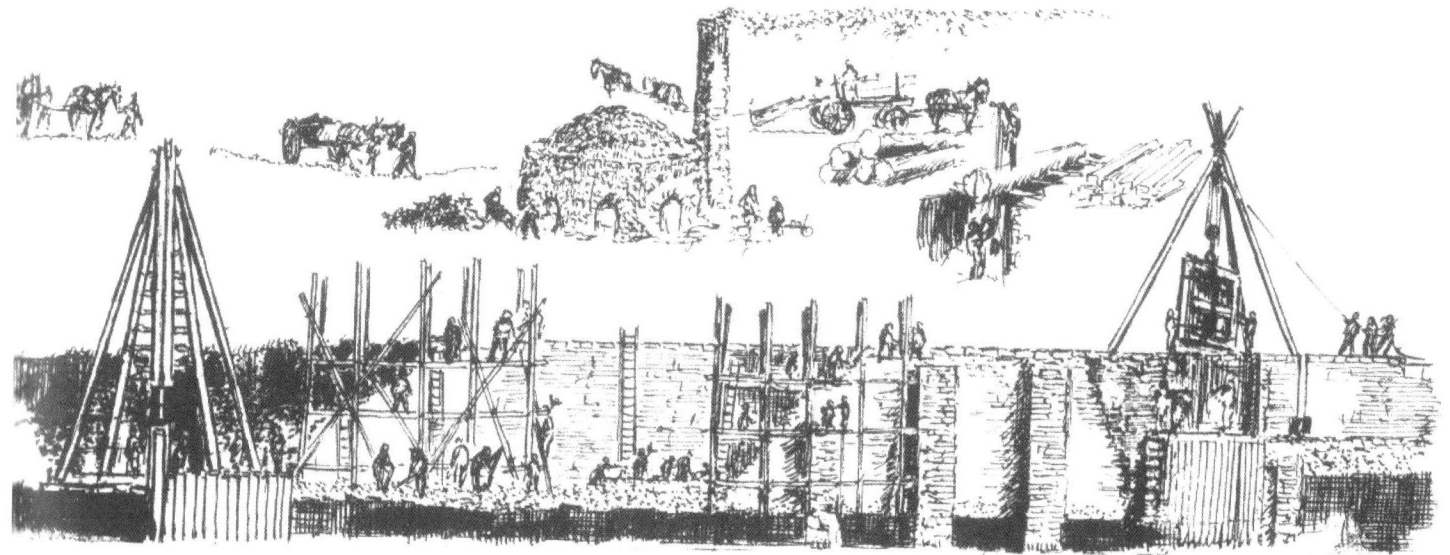

Overleaf top and bottom gates are illustrated together for comparison.

By way of contrast, a guillotine gate is also illustrated, *overleaf upper right,* as fitted to the stop lock on the Stratford-upon-Avon Canal at Kings Norton where it joins the Worcester and Birmingham Canal. The guillotine was chosen as the best solution here because the fall of water between the two canals could be either way.

The task of a stop lock was to conserve one canal's water against the other's, but often there was a deliberate fall of say 15cms (6 inches) in one direction so that one canal would always benefit from a boat's passage. Thus the Birmingham Ca-

nal made the Dudley build a stop lock which would keep the Dudley 15cms (6 inches) above the Birmingham.

Gates were made of oak until recent times, when steel replaced all but the breast or mitre post and the heel post, though again even more recently, oak is now used again. Cast iron gates and special paddle gear were fitted to some locks on the Eastern Branch of the Montgomeryshire Canal as early as the 1820s. In contrast, the huge gates on the Manchester Ship Canal are of greenheart timber.

A miscellany of lock features is illustrated *opposite*. Lock chambers have been built out of turf, timber, brick, stone, cast iron and concrete. A turf sided lock *top right* was the simplest, dug out with sloped sides; brick or stone work only being needed for the gate abutments. A guard rail prevented boats grounding. Two of these locks, at Garston near Theale, and at Thatcham, survive on the River Kennet, but those on the River Wey have gone. They were prodigal with water, and the only canal equivalent that comes to mind are the locks on the Stover Canal in Devon.

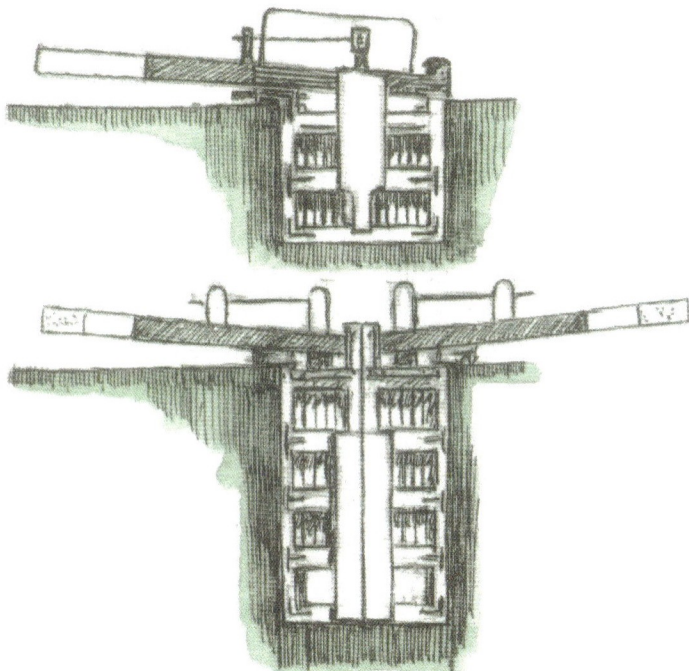

Timber *top left* was confined to flash locks although some brick pound locks in the Midlands have a timber framework along their sides. Brick *top centre* is general in the Midlands and masonry *upper left* in the North and in South Wales. There is a single instance of a cast iron lock at Beeston on the Chester Canal *centre left*, built to cope with the running sand around its foundations. There was also the steel lock at Thurlwood on the Trent and Mersey, essentially a steel tank with jacking points to counter subsidence. It took a long time to fill and has been removed.

Paddle gear is delightfully varied and this selection ranges from the simple to the sophisticated.

On the previous page the *lower right hand illustration* shows one of the hydraulic applications tried on the canals in the early 1970s to ease the task of drawing paddles for the pleasure boater. They have been considered out of harmony with the spirit of the canals and moreover too slow to operate in an emergency, so since the late 1980s they have been replaced by traditional gear. But similar hydraulic equipment has been given a useful future working lift bridges, for instance, on the Llangollen Canal.

The Upper Lode lock on the Severn below Tewkesbury is also shown *lower left* on the previous page. Powered paddle gear is used here, a worm and nut mechanism driving an electric motor. The worm, linked to the paddle, climbs up and down in the housing.

The page opposite shows a miscellany of paddle gear:-

Upper right. Handspike worked rack and pinion gear on the Calder and Hebble Navigation. Used both on gate and ground paddles.

Upper left. Paddle gear on the Wey, a multi holed bar drawn up and held by a peg is fitted to the gates.

Upper centre. Windlass and chain gate paddle gear on the Stover Canal.

Centre (with handle). A jack clough on the Leeds and Liverpool, this is a top ground paddle which swings to one side to open the culvert.

Centre left. Standard rack and pinion gear on a gate on the Shropshire Union.

Centre. Counterbalanced ground paddle gear on the Bridgewater and Taunton.

Centre (with windlass). Horizontal ground paddle gear on the Eastern Branch of the Montgomeryshire. The paddle moves horizontally by means of a toothed sector geared down in two stages from the windlass shaft. The windlass is detachable, a deterrent to tamperers.

Centre right. Worm and nut ground paddle gear as fitted to the new Grand Union locks when the Napton-Birmingham line was improved in the 1930s.

Bottom. A radial clough or paddle on a gate on the Lancaster Canal, worked by rack and pinion with a non-detachable handle.

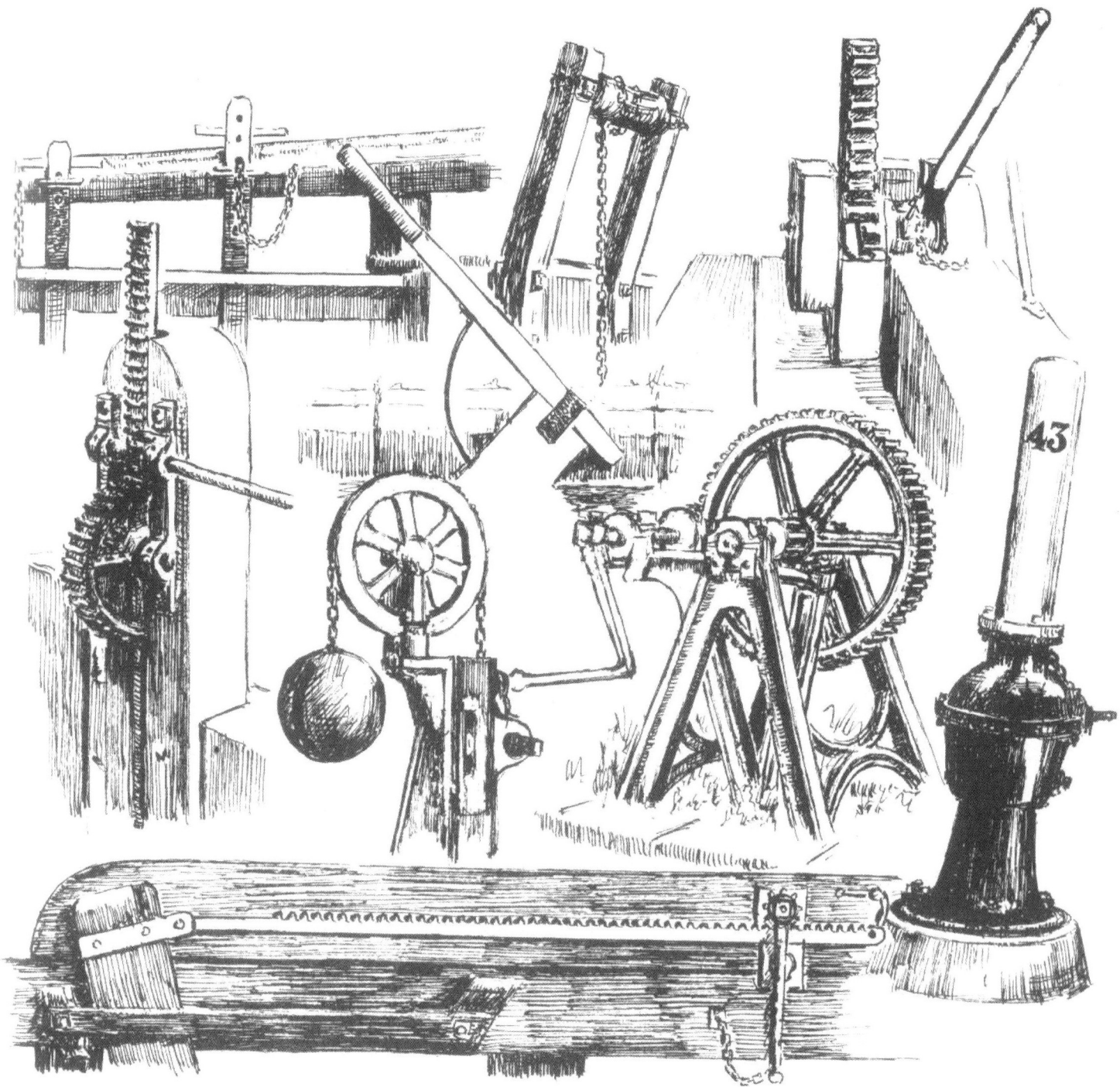

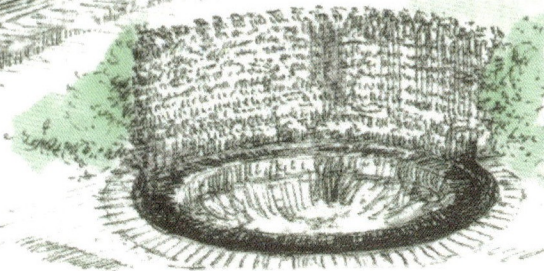

The page *opposite* considers (in clockwise direction) a variety of lock features, large and small.

The two illustrations *top left* show how collars are fitted to hold lock gates into their quoins. Most often the collar passes round the heel post but an alternative (as shown in the upper illustration) is to have the collar encircling an extension piece to the quoin.

Lock keepers might be responsible for several locks. Sometimes they were given huts in which to shelter like this one *top centre* on the Trent and Mersey.

More substantial were lock houses; usually simple cottages, often of a local style like this on the Staffordshire and Worcestershire *top right* it is reached by a bridge across the lock tail. This arrangement is a common feature on this canal - but was awkward as it meant casting off the line when using a horse boat.

Side ponds are a means of economising on lockage water by storing it for re-use. There could be one or two side ponds per lock, although experiments with more were tried. The ponds shown *centre right* are at Marsworth on the Grand Junction.

Large river locks, with continuous traffic, might demand continuous working from the lock keepers, in which case a two family home was needed as at Upper Lode, below Tewkesbury on the Severn *bottom right*.

It is necessary to let off excess water from an upper to a lower pound to stop it spilling over lock gates. One solution is a bywash, a simple sill and spillway leading past the lock to a culvert that discharges water at the lock tail. Excess water bypasses the lock via the spillway and culvert to avoid going over the lock gates and damaging them.

On the Staffordshire and Worcestershire, the sills are, in some instances, circular - funnelling into a culvert. The shape allows a greater discharge. Wire cages like lobster pots can be fitted to keep out debris. Both types of sill are shown *bottom left*.

INCLINED PLANES

Locks could manage any reasonable ascent, but if the climb was particularly steep or if water was scarce, some mechanical means of raising boats might be considered. This was often the best solution if the canal was a small one.

Much ingenuity went into the design of inclined planes and lifts; some were successful, others not. The first inclines were simply chutes carrying goods rather than boats, like these of 1777 on the St Columb Canal near Newquay in Cornwall *below left*. Cut into the cliff they sent stone down to the beach for shipment - while a horse whim wound up boxes of coal, or sea sand (for use as a fertilizer) then to be carried inland by this little canal.

The first English boat plane was that at Ketley in East Shropshire *below right*. Built in 1788, it worked until about 1816. Since the laden traffic was all downhill, from a colliery to iron furnaces, the plane worked by the weight of a descending boat; going down in a wheeled carriage while pulling up another. The rate of descent was controlled by a brake. The evidence for the appearance of the plane comes from a token struck by the Reynolds, the ironworks owners, and from an illustration in William Reynolds' sketch book in which a lock is also visible. There must have been one lock for each track if the boats were to be handled out of the water and onto their cradles.

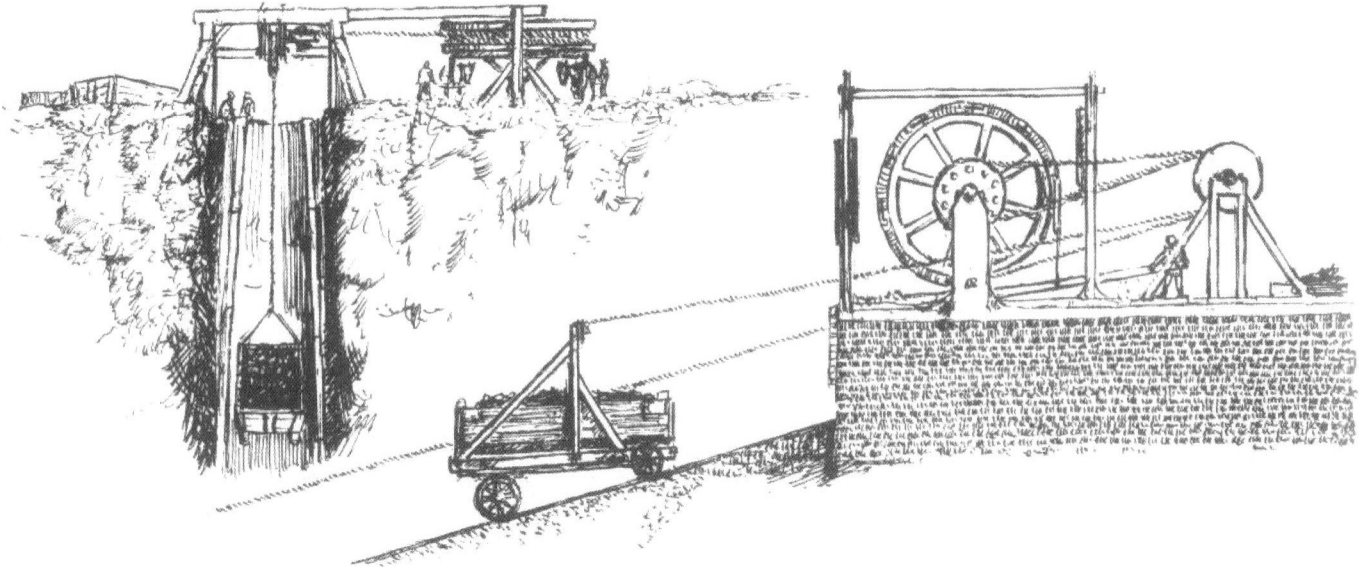

The success at Ketley inspired other planes on the East Shropshire canals. In some cases they would be gravity worked, although others depended on steam power; all had steam engines to pull the boats in and out of the water at the top however. The vessels were small tub boats of 5.1 tonnes (5 ton) capacity, 5.48 metres (18 feet) long and 1.52 metres (5 feet) wide. One of these inclines at The Hay near Coalport has been partially restored at its location within the Blists Hill Industrial Museum complex. It had worked until 1894. At nearby Trench, a plane on the Shrewsbury Canal remained in traffic until 1921. The West of England was another fertile area for incline building. As traffic was not so intense, a different way of working had to be found. Again, small tub boats were used, attached to an endless chain usually powered by a waterwheel - but in one case by a water turbine. This enabled the planes to work whenever a boat or train of boats turned up, and from whatever direction. The boats might be floated in wheeled caissons, or carried "dry" on carriages. In some cases they even had wheels themselves. The illustration *below* shows the plane on the Torrington Canal at Weare Giffard as opened in 1827. There is a photograph of this, so the evidence for the arrangement is conclusive, except for the boats as they are not seen on the photograph. However it is highly probable that they were wheeled. With the waterwheel providing the power, the boats could travel up and down, each attached by a short chain to either the uphill or the downhill side of the endless chain. The Torrington plane stayed in use until about 1871.

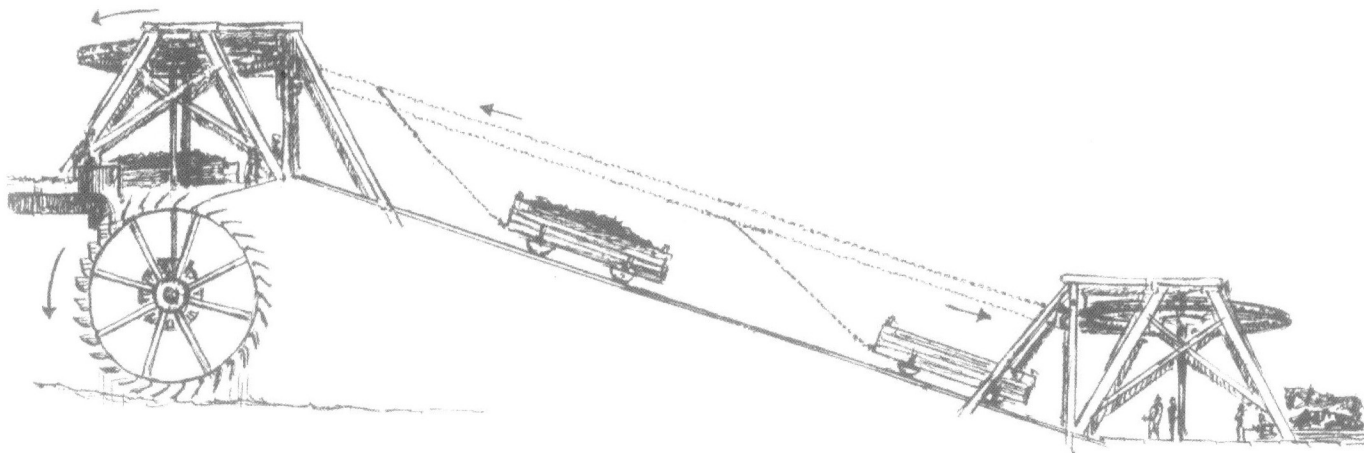

Most venturesome of the West Country tub boat canals was the Bude, in Cornwall. Opened in 1823, it totalled 35.5 miles with its branches, running inland from Bude to not far short of Launceston. On it were six inclined planes for wheeled boats, five worked by waterwheels on the endless chain principle. The sixth at Hobbacott Down was the largest, with a vertical rise of 68 metres (225 feet).

It depended on water filled buckets descending into a well as deep as the rise of the incline. There were two buckets each filled in turn; the full one drew up the empty one so driving an endless cable to which the boats were attached. The buckets held 15.24 tonnes (15 tons) of water and were filled from the canal at the top. At the bottom, a valve was tripped to empty them, and the water then drained into the lower canal. Should the buckets fail (and they often did so) a steam winding engine was available.

In working order, Hobbacott Down illustrated *top opposite* worked well, but the equipment of the time was not really strong enough for the constant usage involved.

Within the technical competence of the period was the Grand Junction's incline at Foxton in Leicestershire; opened in 1900, and illustrated *below opposite*.

The plan was to create a wide boat route from London to the Nottinghamshire-Derbyshire coalfield with an incline to replace the long flight of narrow locks at Foxton. Design and construction of the incline were substantial, with sixteen rails being laid up a concrete ramp; eight for each caisson. 24 metres (80 feet) by 4-5 metres (15 feet) wide, they were able to take either two narrow boats or one wide boat apiece. At the bottom, the caissons descended into the water, while at the top they faced up to two short canal arms closed off by guillotine gates. The caissons likewise were closed with guillotine gates. They were kept in equilibrium by means of a balance and tail rope, and needed only a low horse power engine to move them. This was geared down to a large diameter winding drum.

However, traffic did not justify keeping the boiler in steam, and in 1910 the locks were reopened to all traffic. Today the plane site is under restoration.

CANAL LIFTS

Canal lifts have had a similar history to planes, at first as hoists transferring only goods, then developed to lift boats. A hoist is illustrated *right*, at Hugh's Bridge on the Donnington Wood Canal in East Shropshire. Here a branch canal from limestone quarries ended in a tunnel below the main canal. Both were tub boat routes. The crane transferred the limestone up one shaft in a bucket, assisted by another bucket which descended with the coal that the limekilns needed. This hoist started work in about 1770, but some twenty years later was replaced by a steam worked incline of probably greater capacity.

By the 1790s, experiments with boat lifts were starting but without much success. The most promising was that tried at Tardebigge in 1808, on the Worcester and Birmingham Canal. It worked well, but was not thought strong enough for regular traffic.

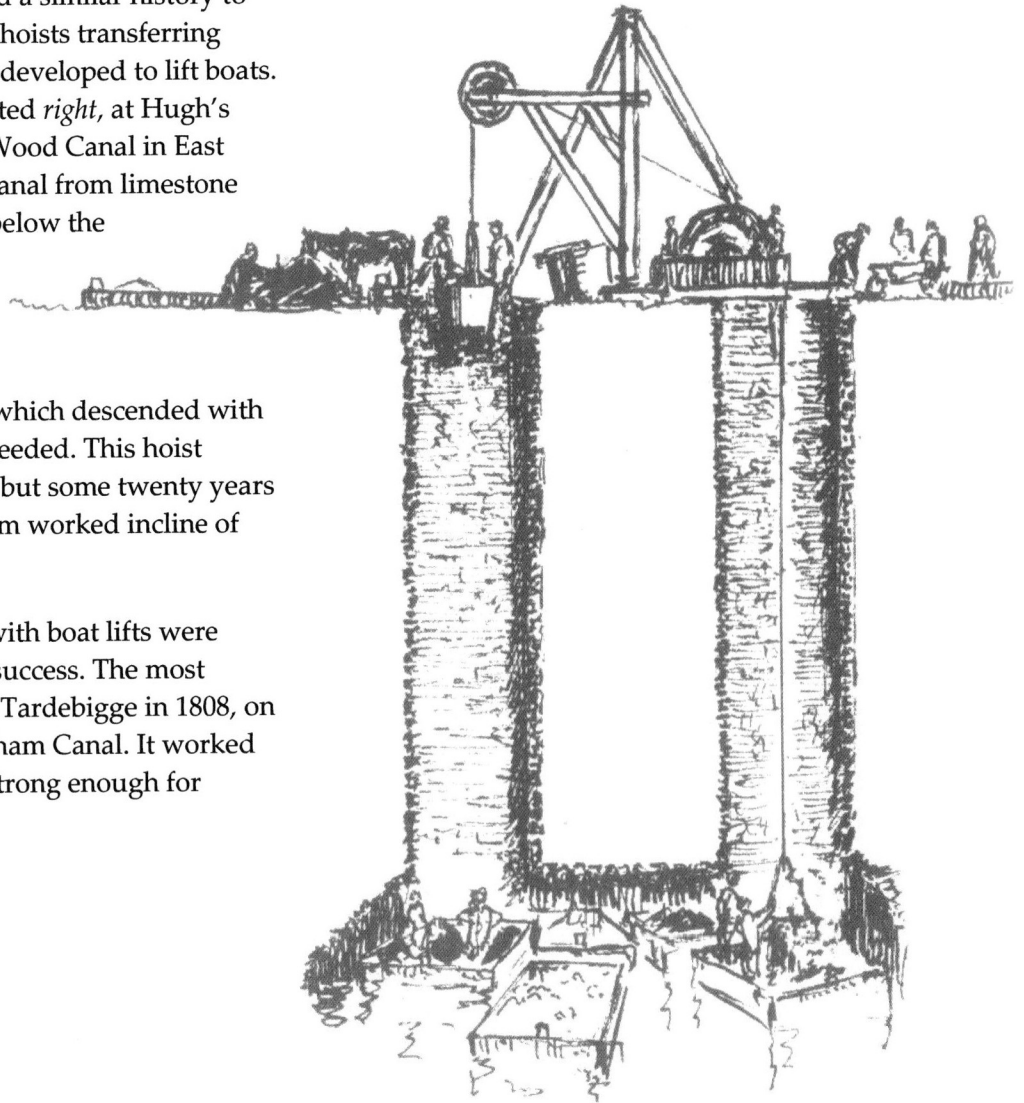

Again it was in the hilly West Country that the lift flourished. Seven were installed on the Grand Western Canal's Taunton extension opened in 1838; another tub boat line. They worked *right* by means of counterbalancing caissons in which the boats floated. Movement was made possible by the weight supplied by the addition of 5cms (2 inches) of water to the upper caisson, while descent was controlled by a brake, assisted if needs be by hand gear. Counterbalancing was made possible by chains hanging down from the caissons that balanced the lifting chains. There were teething troubles over the floating out of the boats at the lower level and for some of the lifts a lock had to be provided; but on the whole they all worked well and remained in service until 1867. Much of the stonework of the lift at Nynehead near Wellington still remains; enough to make its operation understandable.

As at Foxton, advances in technology allowed a lift to be built which could handle the traffic between the Weaver and the Trent and Mersey Canal 15 metres (50 feet) above. It was sited where both river and canal came close; at Anderton near Northwich, opposite the then new Brunner Mond chemical works at Winnington. Anderton has had a long history of transhipment. Ever since the Trent and Mersey opened there was a growing array of chutes and hoists. The lift was the culmination of such efforts to transfer cargoes with greater efficiency.

Opened in 1875, it originally worked hydraulically *left hand illustration opposite* with the two caissons, each able to hold two narrow boats, or alternatively one wide boat. Supported by hydraulic rams, the descending caisson forced up the ascending one via a linking pipe (which for some reason the original plan and hence the illustration does not show). In order to work, the descending caisson had to be heavier, so 15 cms (6 inches) of water were added to it from the canal. When it reached the bottom and dropped into the river additional hydraulic power from an accumulator had to bring the top caisson to canal level; in the illustration the accumulator is to the left and the pump and boiler house are to the right. The bottom caisson had to lose its 15cms (6 inches) of water and the top one had to gain the same amount for the operation to begin again.

All went well until, in 1882, one of the cylinders burst and both had to be renewed. Then by 1905 both these cylinders and the rams were found to be corroded and scored by acid pollution from the chemical works. It was evident that they would need replacing so the Weaver Trustees, who had already converted the guillotine gates and accumulator to electric power, decided to equip the lift itself with electric motors. By building a gantry over the hydraulic lift, they allowed the latter to carry on working as shown in the *right hand illustration*. This gantry carried all the gearing and pulleys and motors needed. Now the caissons could work independently with counterweights 254 tonnes (250 tons) balancing each tank. Employing 1800:1 reduction gearing allowed an electric motor of only thirty horse power to be used for each tank.

The conversion was finished by 1908 and the lift stayed operable until 1986, latterly used by pleasure craft. It is now in need of restoration, the framework having deteriorated to an unacceptable level which forced the closure. The future of the lift remains the subject of much debate, but restoration is anticipated.

[Publisher's note: major restoration work commenced in 2000, and the lift was reopened to boat traffic in 2002. It is now a very popular visitor destination, and is a Scheduled Monument.]

CROSSING THE WATERWAY

The first indication of a canal sighted across the fields is often a humped bridge; humped because although the road was there first, it then had to climb over the newcomer. River bridges are usually old established crossings, with newer structures sometimes replacing the old, and built in new materials. Canals imposed bridges where none had existed before. They were compelled to make them by their Parliamentary Acts - so that roads could remain intact, and landowners and farmers suffered minimum inconvenience when their land was divided. Many therefore were accommodation bridges, such as this on the Shropshire Union *top opposite*. The span has to cross both the canal and towpath, with the canal narrowed to a single boat's width to save expense. Designs were often standardised on each canal.

Cheaper to provide was an opening bridge; just a simple abutment and no need to cross the towpath, while the span itself could be quite light if only to be used by cattle, sheep and the occasional cart. Tractors were not yet in evidence. The Oxford Canal has some distinctive lifting or bascule bridges *centre right* which when lifted, roll back with a toothed sector engaging a horizontal rack. The turnover bridge *centre left* is specific to canals by which the towpath changed sides. It was so designed that the horse's line need not be un-hitched, this achieved by making each of the approach ramps on each bank on the same side of the bridge. This turnover or "changeline" bridge is on the Peak Forest Canal at Marple.

Providing an uninterrupted way for towpaths demanded much ingenuity; they had to cross arms and branches by side bridges, while at junctions give unhindered passage to horses in all the directions required. Working locks was speedier and safer if there was a bridge over the lock tail. An overall bridge meant unhitching the towline, gathering it up and passing it through - but if a gap was left in the span, the line could be dropped through. Such split bridges were provided on the Stratford Canal and also, as illustrated later, on the Trent and Mersey.

Considerable bridge works were asked of the Manchester Ship Canal, especially in the provision of deviations for the railways, notably in the Warrington area. The lines had to cross at least 20 metres up (over 70 feet), clear of masts and funnels on not too punitive a gradient. Illustrated *bottom right* is the Latchford viaduct that carries the Warrington-Stockport line over the ship canal.

In the same way as many canal companies built their masonry accommodation bridges to a standard design - so also were cast iron bridges standardised in some industrial areas.

The Birmingham Canal Navigations employed a standard design *below* from the Horseley Iron-works at Tipton. A similar bridge was also found, albeit with a different pattern of railings, on the northern Oxford when it was shortened in the 1830s. The scene illustrated here is at Windmill End where the Netherton tunnel line meets the Dudley Canal. This bridge is actually over the Boshboil Arm.

Even the humble masonry accommodation bridge *top right opposite* had to be designed and built with care. An arch was usually needed to achieve the span over canal and path and because the whole construction was above ground

Level, care had to be taken to avoid settlement under the weight of the approach road. The solution was not only to slope (or "batter") the face walls of the bridge but to curve them out from the centre, giving an arch shape in plan also, which helped provide resistance to lateral pressure. The arch over the canal was built up on wooden centring, about three courses of brickwork thick, then rubble-filled up to the roadbed.

If a road approached the canal at an oblique
angle, early engineers preferred to modify its
route to give a right angled crossing of the canal,
but by the late 1780s skew bridges were
introduced. These had winding courses to
give the brick arch bottom right the spiral effect
necessary to complete the span at an angle.
A notably skewed brick bridge has been preserved
at Monkhide on the route of the now abandoned
[publisher's note: but subject to restoration work]
Herefordshire and Gloucestershire Canal.

Not only were opening bridges cheaper than the fixed variety, but if ships were involved the problems of providing high clearance were solved. Either the bridge could lift, or it could swing. *Opposite* is illustrated a selection of lifting and bascule bridges.

First at the *top* comes the largest bascule bridge in the British Isles, over the Trent at Keadby. Opened in 1916, it carries the Doncaster-Scunthorpe line of the former Great Central Railway as well as a main road. The 18 metre (20 yards) opening span rolled back as it lifted, the whole bridge being 134 metres (440 feet) long. Design was by the American Scherzer Rolling Lift Bridge Company, using the same principles as the far smaller Oxford Canal lifting bridges described earlier. Two one hundred and fifteen horse power electric motors, aided by counterweights, were used to raise the Keadby bascule; but today it is fixed. Modern low air draught ships can easily pass beneath the span.

Still in use on Ramsden's Canal is the Turnbridge in Huddersfield illustrated *centre right*. This was completed in 1865. Hand worked, it is one of several designs of vertical lift bridge. Others include the electric powered example at Litherland on the Leeds and Liverpool Canal and another at Royston on the Barnsley Canal. Counterweights dropping down columns aid operation of this Huddersfield bridge.

Counter weighting was also the means of working the well known lift bridges on the Llangollen Canal. Most of these span minor tracks, but that at Wrenbury, *centre left*, by Arthur Sumner's former corn mill takes a fair amount of road traffic - so it was given a windlass rather than a simple chain. Nowadays it employs hydraulic gear. The inner ends of the beam support the box of weights, made up of concrete and scrap metal. Other canals have similar bridges; the Caldon, the Stratford, and the Northampton branch of the Grand Junction, while in South Wales there was an unusual one *bottom* at Newport on the Monmouthshire. This carried a rail siding at an angle to the Cordes Dos Nail Works, which is why there were two leaves to the bridge.

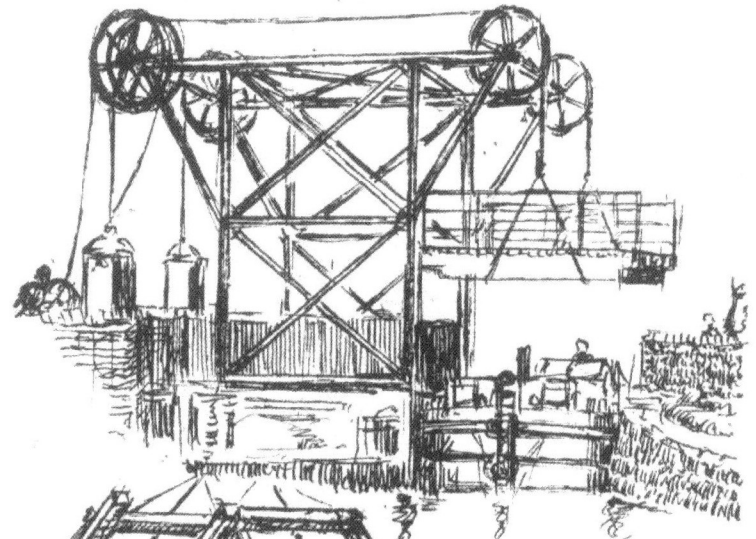

Swing bridges also gained a clear opening - and as a result were widespread. They too had the advantage of cheapness, needing less of an abutment than a lifting span, simply requiring a foundation for the turntable. They were used on the Sankey Brook Navigation (to allow sailing flats to come up) as well as on the Macclesfield, the Peak Forest, the Cromford, the Basingstoke and the Grand Junction Canals.

They are most numerous on the Leeds and Liverpool *top opposite,* some of wood and some steel, while there is an electrically powered example at Leigh. Tensioning rods stop the span sagging, and they can be tightened by turnbuckles.

On the Gloucester and Sharpness *centre opposite,* to allow clearance for ships, all the bridges swing - except for the recent lift bridge at Gloucester. Up to 1963 they were double span which meant a "passman" had to cycle along the towpath to open and close the offside spans. The bridge keepers who lived in elegant Regency bridge houses were responsible for the nearside. Illustrated is the bridge at Frampton, which now like all the others is single span and electrically powered.

Large hydraulically operated swing bridges provide most of the road crossings of the Manchester Ship Canal, while there are road and rail swing bridges over the Ouse at Selby, and electric swing bridges over the Weaver. The illustration *bottom opposite* shows the one at Sutton Weaver cut away to show the floating pontoon that turns with the bridge. The drive cables to the winch beneath the bridge house are also seen. A floating pontoon needs less power to turn, as well as countering subsidence.

On the two following pages comes more bridge variety:-

Overleaf top left is one of the lock bridges on the Watford flight of the Grand Union line to Leicester.

Overleaf top right is the ornamental Avenue Bridge on the Shropshire Union near Brewood. It carries the drive to Chillington Hall, the seat of the Gifford family. In common with many bridges in the vicinity of great estates, it was ornately embellished to satisfy the vanities of the landowners.

Overleaf centre right is the famous towpath bridge at Great Haywood where the Trent and Mersey meets the Staffordshire and Worcester Canal. Its elegant form has been the inspiration for a bridge over the nearby M6.

Overleaf bottom left is illustrated one of the cast iron skew bridges built by the London and Birmingham Railway over the Grand Junction Canal. The illustration shows a London and North Western "Jumbo" locomotive with a down express. These engines were driven hard and noisily to the terror of the boat horse at work below.

It was Leeds and Liverpool practice *top* not only to whitewash the bridge arch but to add a vertical stroke to mark the centre of the channel; both would show up in a headlight.

Canal bridges were built before the age of the traction engine and few were strong enough to bear their weight. The weight restriction signs *bottom right* went up as a result of the Motor Car Acts of 1896 and 1903.

NOTICE
THIS
BRIDGE

HEAVYMOTORCAR

THREETONS

FIVETONS

TRAILER

TRAILER
FIVETONS

ALONG THE TOWPATH

Towpath maintenance in the days of horse traction was given at least as much consideration as care of the water channel. The composite scene *below* includes hedge layering, spreading stone chippings or "raffle" and piling the bank by driving in the piles with a 561b (25kg) sledge hammer - all tasks essential for the upkeep of a sound and easily useable path. Spoil is being tipped from the cart to make up the camber of the towpath. This was sloped down from the canal edge so that the horses had a better purchase, with the path angled away from the canal. The edge of the path was normally some two feet above the water level.

Because tolls were charged by the mile it was necessary to mark distances carefully. *Opposite* is a selection of such mileposts, while a couple of boundary posts as used to mark the property limits of the canal companies' territory are also illustrated. These boundary examples from the River Weaver Navigation *top centre* and the Birmingham Canal Navigations *bottom centre* are both of cast iron - as were many of the mileposts used.

FROM POTTER STREET LOCK
9
MILE
M.C.C°

RWN

LEEDS 32 MILES

L'POOL 95 MILES

WALBRIDGE 17½

INGLESHAM 11

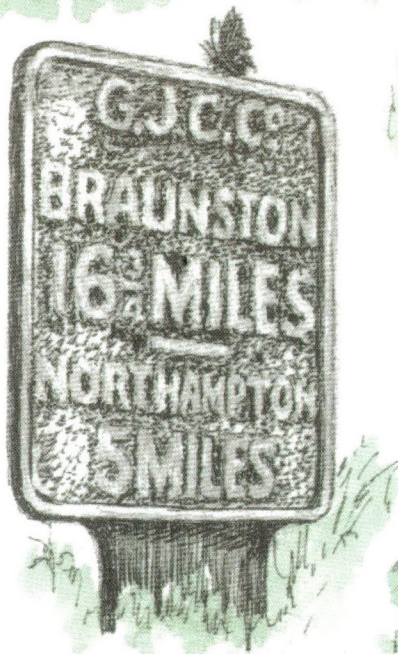

G.J.C.C°
BRAUNSTON
16¾ MILES
NORTHAMPTON
5 MILES

B.C
N

AUTHERLEY JUNCTION 23 MILES

NANTWICH 16 MILES

NORBURY JUNCTION 7 MILES

Horse traction demanded precautions on the towpath. The guard rails *top left opposite* had to have the top rail sloped down to the ground to stop the towing lines catching. To provide guidance for tow lines at awkward places, and to reduce the wear on parapets, rollers might be provided like those on the Marple flight on the Peak Forest Canal *top right opposite*. Bridge brickwork and masonry had to be protected against the constant wear of towlines *bottom left opposite*. Although a towing line might only last five or six weeks in service, generations of them *bottom left* cut into the stoutest of protective ironwork. The sharp bends on the summit pound of the Leeds and Liverpool *bottom right* opposite

between Marton and Gargrave had vertical rollers to keep the lines within bounds so that they did not snag, and to ensure an efficient angle of pull.

Working a lock is safer and speedier when there is a bridge over the lock tail. However, an overall bridge would mean unhitching a towline, gathering it up and passing it through. The whole operation could be made faster and simpler if there was a gap in the span through which the line could be dropped. Such split bridges were provided on the Trent and Mersey as illustrated *below,* the Birmingham and Stourbridge Canals - and on the Stratford.

ways" were unsatisfactory in other directions, they were 2.4 metres (8 feet) up on the floodbank and maybe some way from the river's edge. They changed sides without bridges and never passed under bridges. The horses, therefore, had to be ferried over to the appropriate side, either on a boat stationed by the bank for the job, or on the foredeck of a lighter. More conveniently organised was the River Weaver Navigation in Cheshire, which used specially shaped gates *below*, which swung to behind the horse by their weight.

River paths did not necessarily run on land owned by the navigation, and might be broken up by fences and hedges. These would have to be crossed by stiles *above* or pierced by gates to allow personnel and horses to pass. There were stiles on the East Anglian navigations such as the Suffolk Stour, one being the subject of John Constable's painting "The Leaping Horse". They were supposed to be to a standard 75cms (2 feet 6 inches) high. East Anglian towpaths or "haling

Among the improvements made to the Birmingham Canal system in the 1830s was the provision of twin towpaths on the then new main line from Birmingham to Wolverhampton, and also on the Netherton tunnel line. Illustrated here are the towpaths passing under the Tividale aqueduct which carries the Old Main Line. It is self evident how twin paths would ease congestion and help cope with heavy traffic; no heaving up or dropping of tow lines but a strictly kept rule of the road. Both Coseley and Netherton tunnels were also provided with twin paths. The hut by the aqueduct above is a toll office of the usual BCN island pattern. On the other side of the aqueduct was a small hydroelectric plant that supplied nearby cottages.

WATER SUPPLY

Much as a steam locomotive requires coal and a motor car requires petrol or diesel, so also a canal requires water if it is to fulfil its function and carry boats up and down its length. Each time a lock is used a large quantity of water has to be passed down from the summit - a narrow lock requires up to 118,000 litres (approx 26,000 gallons) while a lock on a broad canal can take as much as 254,000 litres (approx 56,000 gallons) to fill. The deeper the lock the greater the volume of water needed.

Rivers depend directly on nature for their water - but in exchange a river navigation authority has to put up with the uncertainties of flood and drought. However, the canal engineers had to ensure that their waterways could receive adequate supplies of water, artificially channelled or pumped in - and in sufficient quantities to allow for the expected volumes of traffic on their route. Without sufficient water the canal could not be operated. No wonder the Canal companies used stop locks to ensure that their water did not pass to their neighbours.

The ultimate source of water for both rivers and canals is, of course rain; rain which feeds streams, rivers and lakes - and, via natural and constructed channels, the reservoirs and feeders on which the canals directly depend. Rain also provides for the wells and springs from which some canals may draw their supplies - while both land drainage and water pumped up from mines are further sources.

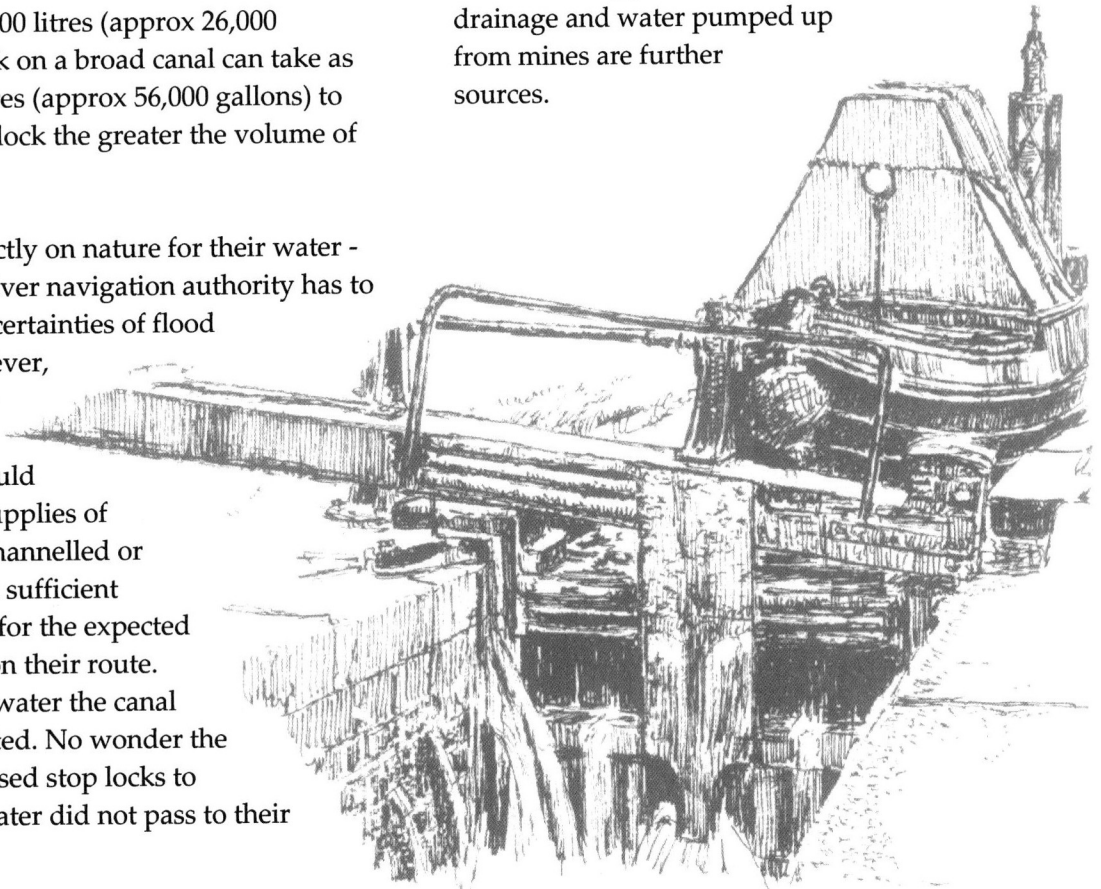

Water consumption is not just caused by boats locking down from the summit. Evaporation and the transpiration of plants, weeds and rushes consume some - and there is always leakage and percolation through the banks of even the best managed canal, the consequence of burrowing by water rats, moles and rabbits. Cattle drinking from the bank side use water - a single fattening animal consumes 35 litres (8 gallons) a day - while dairy cows *above* need even more.

Locks, *opposite*, can leak heavily if in poor condition while waste weirs can deteriorate, thus releasing more water than they should. Water losses of this kind can account for up to 4cms (nearly 2 inches) a day over the whole surface of the canal - without a single boat moving. For the majority of canals, reservoirs are the crucial means of ensuring the supply of water needed over the year - storing what falls as winter rain for later use. In a hot summer much of the rain that falls will be discounted by the daily losses described above.

The site for a reservoir will usually be selected in the light of the adequacy of its feeders - the streams feeding in from the catchment area. In many cases a natural valley site impounded by a headbank or dam is sufficient to retain the quantities of water needed - though in the flatter areas of the Midlands it was often necessary to build shallower reservoirs with their contents retained behind artificial embankments. Both the headbanks and any such embankments had to be waterproof, as well as strong enough to resist the lateral pressure of thousands of gallons of water. Generally they would be built using the same techniques as for a canal embankment. A puddle bottom together with puddle ditches down the sides would be incorporated as needed to contain any leaks. Each reservoir was designed to provide for the anticipated needs of its own section of the canal, its expected traffic being converted into lockfuls of water. Against these needs, calculations on the quantity of local supplies available from rain, streams, land drainage and other sources would be made - and a reservoir of adequate size constructed.

But in many cases, as traffic levels increased, canals found the capacity of their original reservoirs too small. The Trent and Mersey is a case in point - for despite the water obtained from mine drainage at Harecastle and from a reservoir at Stanley that fed into the main route along the Caldon branch, still more capacity was needed by the closing years of the eighteenth century. The immediate solution lay in the opening of Rudyard, *right*, the particular characteristics of which can be used to explain the general features of water supply via such a reservoir.

The panoramic illustration *opposite* shows the headbank at Rudyard above Leek, completed in 1802 to supply the Trent and Mersey via the newly opened branch to Leek. The headbank here is some 160 metres (175 yards) long and 58 metres (64 yards) wide at the base. The cutaway shows how the outlet works. It starts as a pipe from a strainer box below the top of the headbank. The strainer prevents debris from entering the pipework. This pipe is fitted with a main valve worked by worm and nut gear. The pipe then splits into two, each with a wheel valve for finer control of the rate of discharge into the culvert which opens onto a lagoon. Excess water passes over a fixed weir. The lagoon, some 40 metres long acts as a settling pond. One side and one end are sills over which the canal feed passes, but before it can do this compensation water is taken through a slot weir and returned to the Churnet to make up for water which the canal takes from this river. The slot will take exactly the amount calculated as compensation, the lagoon ensuring that there is no head of water to force extra through the slot. When the slot is satisfied, feed to the canal may start. This is measured over a sharp edged gauging weir, the gauge calibrated in megalitres per day (a megalitre is a million litres).

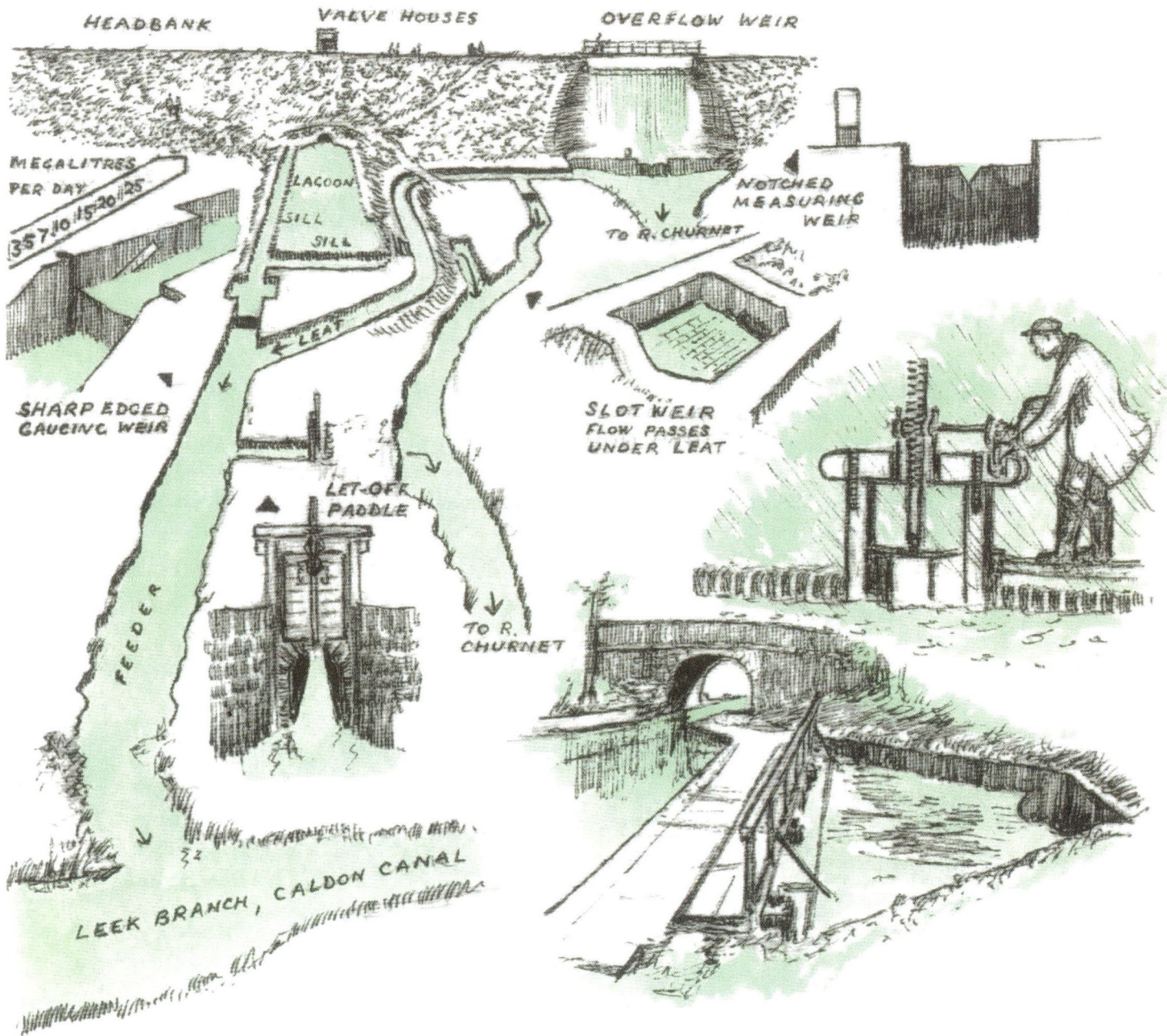

HEADBANK   VALVE HOUSES   OVERFLOW WEIR

MEGALITRES
PER DAY

3 5 7 10 15 20 25

LAGOON
SILL
SILL

NOTCHED
MEASURING
WEIR

TO R. CHURNET

LEAT

SHARP EDGED
GAUGING WEIR

SLOT WEIR
FLOW PASSES
UNDER LEAT

LET-OFF
PADDLE

TO R.
CHURNET

FEEDER

LEEK BRANCH, CALDON CANAL

Water coming down the overflow weir passes over another measuring weir with a notch in it which can thus record the tiniest trickle. It too flows into the River Churnet. Once over its measuring weir, the canal feed continues down to the Leek branch by a three mile artificial channel. There is a let-off paddle down its course should it become overfull.

The feed into a canal may be by a pipe, weir or a simple junction of water as is the Rudyard feeder. However there are times when a canal is overfull, threatening the banks. Normally waste weirs take care of the level, the longer the sill the more able the weir is to dispose of the water. An example is at Denford on the Leek branch of the Caldon, not far from the Rudyard feeder. In an emergency, and able to release water at a great rate, a flood or let-off paddle has to be drawn.

Usually they were made like a lock paddle with a three sided spindle end which only the lock keeper or lengthsman's windlass would fit. Turning out in pouring rain in the middle of the night as illustrated *centre right* on the *previous page* was not unusual. Nowadays the accent is on longer weirs which do the job automatically.

While the bulk of reservoirs are above the summit level and feed into these by gravity, some were built to supply lower pounds. An example is the Burnley pound of the Leeds and Liverpool. Additionally there are reservoirs which take water coming down the locks and store it for use in dry spells, pumping it back to the summit, as used to be done at Tardebigge on the Worcester and Birmingham Canal. Some reservoirs take surplus water from other reservoirs and feed into a lower pound, while there are compensation reservoirs which feed back water abstracted from rivers by the canal. There are five of these on the Worcester and Birmingham, originally built for the benefit of mills on the Rivers Rea and Arrow - the rule being that reservoirs should leave unhindered any flow of water which existed before their construction.

Similarly, compensation feeders may supply nearby mills as from the Rochdale Canal *left* to Littleborough.

It was sometimes possible for a canal to take water direct from a river, as the Ellesmere (or Welsh Canal) does from the Dee at Llangollen. The Horseshoe Falls above the town were built for this task. The line from here, by which the river feed comes down to the canal at Trevor, is technically described as a navigable feeder, for although used by boats it was not built to canal width and has a considerable current. The flow continues on more modestly as the canal drops down to Hurleston and to the Shropshire Union main line.

The Brecknock and Abergavenny Canal takes water from the Usk at Brecon, while in Taunton the Bridgewater and Taunton taps the River Tone above Firepool lock. The weir here is on two levels to ensure a constant supply should the river be low. In the foreground of the illustration *above* is a flood paddle which discharges below this weir should the canal become overfull.

Pumping played a big part in the water supply of many canals, for example on the Grand Junction, as the reservoirs at Tring could not be built higher than the canal itself. Pumps were needed to draw water from springs and wells, from mines, to return lockage water and to draw it from rivers.

Occasionally wind pumps were used. The illustration *opposite left* shows that at Thameshead on the Thames and Severn, which worked for only two years from 1790. Wind was found too chancy and would often fail just when it was wanted.

Waterwheel driven pumps were more certain, and those at Claverton fed the Kennet and Avon from their installation in 1810 to 1952. They are now restored *centre opposite* and work again, but reliance is placed on electric pumps here to lift water forty eight feet up from the Avon.

Notably, however, steam engines powered pumps and had a widespread application before they were supplanted by diesel and electricity. Many millions of gallons per year - in some cases for periods of more than a century - have been pumped by beam engines built on the principles established by Thomas Newcomen and James Watt. Originally developed in the early eighteenth century to extract water from mines, these massive engine houses, *right*, with protruding beams

rocking up and down to power the pumps, have been striking features of the canal landscape since the 1830s.

Several notable examples are preserved; those at Crofton on the Kennet and Avon, and at Lea Wood on the Cromford Canal - while the venerable Smethwick engine, first preserved by the Birmingham Canal Navigation at their Ocker Hill workshops, is now in Thinktank, Birmingham, where it may be seen at work. It is the oldest working engine in the world.

Such engines, working with low steam pressures, were simple and reliable, while the up and down reciprocating motion of their beams made them particularly well adapted to the working of pumps. Longevity was another of their characteristics. One such engine, believed to have been built at some time in the 1720s, pumped water from Warwickshire mines for nearly a century before being moved to Hawkesbury Junction. Here, where the Coventry Canal is joined by the Oxford, it continued in occasional work until just before World War I.

There are two engines at Crofton, one dating from 1812 and the other from 1846. They both work on the Cornish cycle and were in regular use here until 1952. A detail of a beam end from a Crofton engine is shown *above right*. Subsequently they have been restored and are regularly steamed.

These older pumps were reciprocating, but later pumps - driven at first by steam, then diesel motors and now by electricity - are centrifugal and able to pump at much greater rates. A modern 460 mm (18 inch) bore centrifugal submersible pump can deliver 200 - 270 litres (approx 50 gallons) per second. They are fitted with automatic controls and cooled by the water both around them and passing through them. This means that their motors need not be so big - nor are as expensive to run - as those fitted to pumps designed to work out of water.

MAINTAINING THE NAVIGATIONS

Rivers and canals cannot be made ready for boats and then forgotten. Nature, climate and everyday wear and tear all contribute to the ongoing deterioration of a waterway, which will need constant maintenance if it is to remain in a safe and navigable condition.

The natural growth of weeds in the water and of hedges and trees along the towpath need regular attention - while the burrowing of water rats, rabbits and moles can undermine the banks. Floods, likewise, can damage river banks, while severe drought can cause the puddle lining of a canal to dry and crack. Frost or carelessly handled boats can damage lock chambers while the lock gates and paddle gear need maintenance and occasional replacement. Weed blocked culverts need clearing out as does the rubbish so often dumped in urban canals - while dredging to remove silt and maintain navigable depth is an ongoing requirement of most waterways.

Such maintenance work is the responsibility of the local engineers, inspectors and staff - the latter involving a host of trades; carpenters, blacksmiths, painters, fitters and electricians. Crane and dredger drivers will work the length of a waterway while lengthsmen, with responsibility for a particular section, will be skilled in puddling, hedging, ditching, weed cutting and bank maintenance. Some canal companies built them houses near their work, for example the round ones on the Thames and Severn of which that at Chalford is illustrated *below*.

Central to maintenance are the repair yards where plant and materials are kept, and where workshops make lock gates, paddle and sluice gear, fittings for swing and lift bridges, doors and window frames for lock cottages - and the like. Big canals needed several yards. The Shropshire Union had Norbury, Chester and Ellesmere, with lock gate making centred on Ellesmere and boat

building on Chester. The Aire and Calder had their main depot at Stanley Ferry with another at Goole, where boats were repaired. Smaller canals had a single yard, like Hartshill *above* on the Coventry Canal near Atherstone. With its turret clock in the cupola, it is more reminiscent of the stables of a great estate than an industrial building.

Weed is a natural hazard, especially on a still water canal; the species ranging from reeds to Algae, and demanding different treatments. Illustrated from *top left to right* are examples of emergent narrow leaved plants. Reed Sweet Grass (Glyceria), widespread on the canals; the Common Reed (Phragmites), even more widespread except on fast flowing rivers. Of emergent broad leaved plants, Arrowhead (Sagittaria) is limited to canals and drainage channels, while of submerged varieties, Canadian Pond Weed (Elodea) is found in still water all over England, and Duckweed (Lemna) builds up into green floating masses. Finally comes Blanket Weed, a filamentous algae which forms scum-like floating masses.

Combating weed invasion can involve pesticides (nowadays frowned upon), cutting - which removes weed but by its pruning action encourages further growth and drowning out emergent weeds which depend on sunlight. To combat algae, a newer technique involves throwing bales of straw into the water; their decay checks growth. Loose straw in a plastic tube is equally effective.

Once, cutting was by hand scythe *centre left*, or by a chain of scythe blades, some twenty or so being linked together *centre right* and jiggled or joggled (the term actually used) back and forth across the canal; a method not seen nowadays. The older paddle driven weed cutting boat *below right* with a V shaped cutter has also been supplanted. It could go in either direction, more usually trailing the cutter as illustrated, but for heavy root growth it led in the closed V position. A modern cutter boat like the Wilder "Water Warrior" *bottom left* has an hydraulic arm mounting a U shaped cutting head which can cope with virtually all weed species.

But weeds are not the only naturally accumulating material that requires removal from waterways. Silt, washed down from the banks or carried in suspension by the drainage waters entering a canal or river constantly builds up. Dredging a canal requires a heavy outlay on equipment - the greater part of the expense incurred, not so much by dredging as by the costs of spoil removal. Whereas the scour of a river's current can clear silt, a still water canal can only be dredged by mechanical means.

The first task is a survey across the channel, sounding from a boat. Sounding poles used to be employed, some 3 metres (18 feet) long graduated in feet and quarter inches with a board or disc nailed to their foot to stop penetration into the silt.

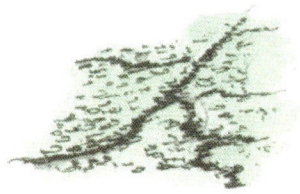

The boat was worked across along a rope stretched from bank to bank, and tagged at 1.5 metre (5 feet) intervals. Soundings were taken at these points, resulting in a cross section of the depth. Now echo sounders and position finding instruments are used but the result is the same; a picture of the underwater scene. Dredgers too work from side to side. If on a river they were to work with the current, the result would be like a ploughed field.

Scoop or spoon dredgers, *top right opposite*, evolved from the techniques once used to dredge sand and gravel for ships' ballast. A long handled iron scoop, pierced with holes to allow drainage, is supported by a crane. Using the cross bar at the end of the handle, the operator can manipulate the scoop underwater, as well as using it to unload the spoil into the hold of the boat. Such dredgers, some with steam powered cranes, lasted into the 1950s.

The grab which has now superseded them, was introduced to canal work in 1896 by the firm of Grafton and Co of Bedford. The "Grafton" *left opposite* used a steam crane to handle the boom that carried the grab. Great accuracy of dredging is possible using grabs of this type.

< 5FT >

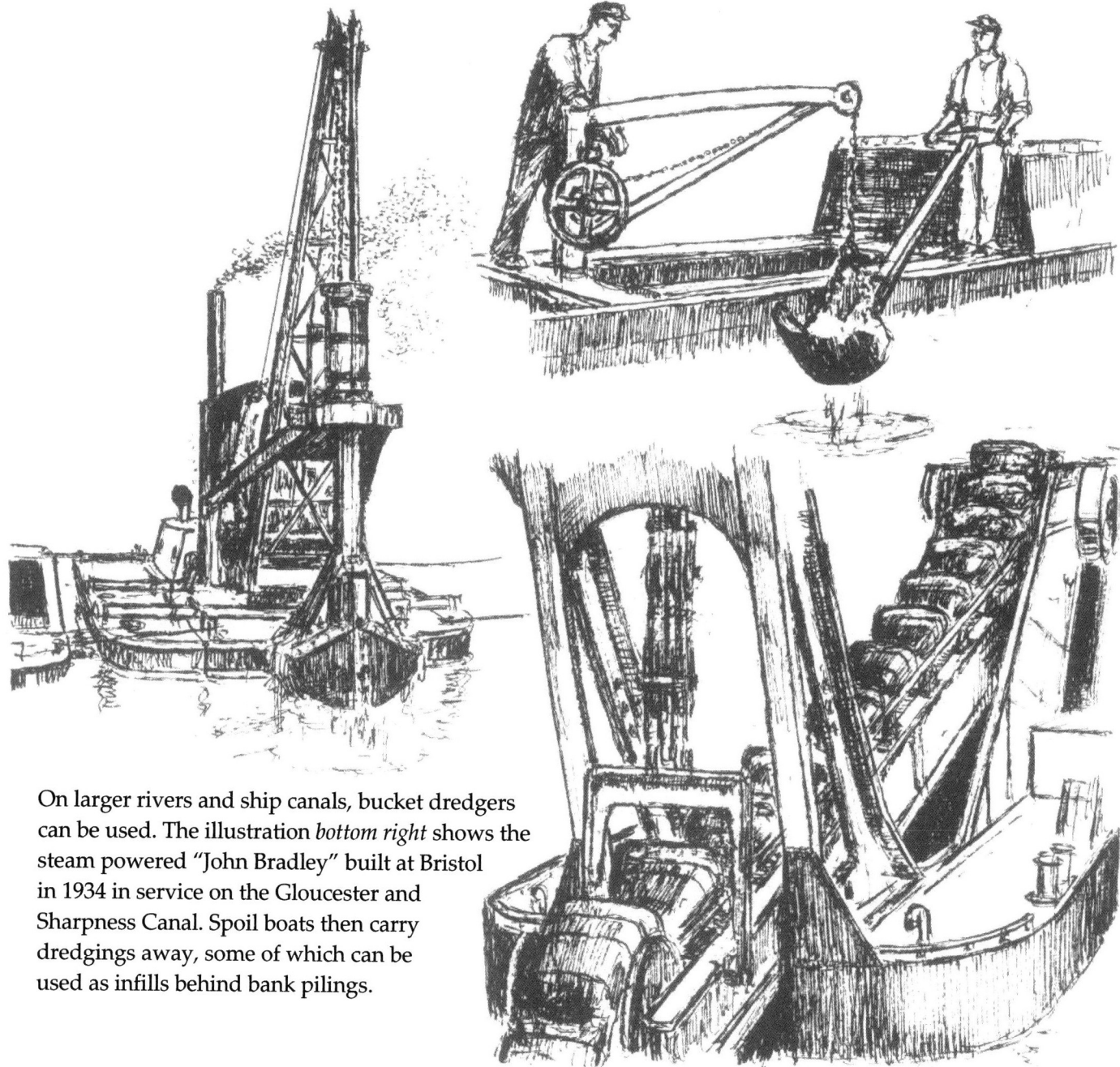

On larger rivers and ship canals, bucket dredgers can be used. The illustration *bottom right* shows the steam powered "John Bradley" built at Bristol in 1934 in service on the Gloucester and Sharpness Canal. Spoil boats then carry dredgings away, some of which can be used as infills behind bank pilings.

A leak from a canal becomes a burst *below* if not quickly checked. Burrowing animals must take some of the blame for leaks; moles, rabbits and particularly water rats weaken banks. It is easy to see where a leak emerges, but discovering where it starts may involve trenching along the bank *centre, opposite*; repairs and repuddling may then be a simple job.

To guard against a burst emptying a long pound, gates are fitted at strategic points, particularly at the ends of embankments where bursts can be most damaging. There is such a stop gate at Nantwich *far left opposite*.

Aqueducts are similarly protected. Gates were fitted in these during the Second War in case of bomb damage, while in areas like Birmingham, where flooding from the extensive canal system was a particular risk, great care was taken to enable the isolation of sections of canal.

Stop planks *centre bottom opposite* are put down for repairs to bridges, tunnels and aqueducts, and can be dropped into place in an emergency. They are stored in racks or recesses *right bottom opposite*. The Kennet and Avon example shown used lengths of fish bellied tramroad rail to store the planks.

Stop planks slide down grooves in side walls on the canal edge, and bed down on a sill. Both the grooves and the sill need to be cleaned out before they are fitted. The planks are held down by Wedges, and against water pressure by a stank bar driven into the canal bed and supported by a longitudinal plank. Leaks between the planks are checked by shovelling in ashes on the water side; this is known as "racking off".

To repair a breach or burst, the canal had to be dammed or stanked off, using the nearest set of stop planks, but to keep traffic moving it was sometimes possible to build a cofferdam round the site of the breach and refill the canal. The illustration *below* shows a burst on the Grand Union at Weedon in 1939 where the traffic problem was solved by piling, strengthened by tieing back to the opposite bank, leaving a channel of a single boat's width. The breach was repaired by

tipping spoil and repuddling the sides and bottom. However if the canal banks are very unstable, more drastic measures might be needed, such as construction of a concrete trough to make a completely self contained channel. This has been done in recent years on the Llangollen line in the Trevor area where much trouble with breaches has been experienced.

Lock repairs often involve attention to brick and stone work, distorted by frost and earth pressure, or damaged by boats. The replacement of gates and sills is also a major task for the maintenance gangs who, whenever possible, do such work in the winter months so that the resultant stoppages have minimum effect on the use of the waterway.

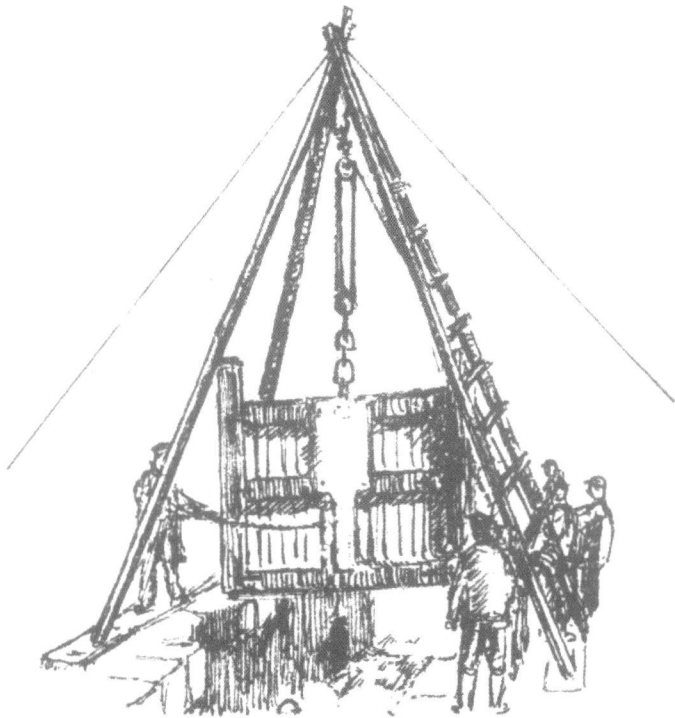

cross beam. When being re-fitted a gate has to be guided by a man on either side of the chamber, with another in the empty lock to ensure that the pivot from the heelpost fits into its recess and the gate rests neatly against the sill.

In recent years demountable gantries *bottom right* have replaced sheerlegs. These can be wheeled into position while the hoist can traverse the steel cross beam. The men take up their traditional positions for this traditional task - but now in hard hats as required by safety legislation.

Sill replacement usually involves the renewal of the upper oak baulk beneath the gates, as the elm below is highly resistant to water and virtually indestructible. But first the gates must be removed - and replaced as necessary. Welded steel was commonly used for gates for a period of time, but wood is normally now used again (partly for heritage reasons).

The illustration *top left* shows sheerlegs being used to lift a gate, the windlass fitted to one set of legs is carrying the load. Gates can be slung or, as shown here, hung from an eyebolt, itself bolted to the top

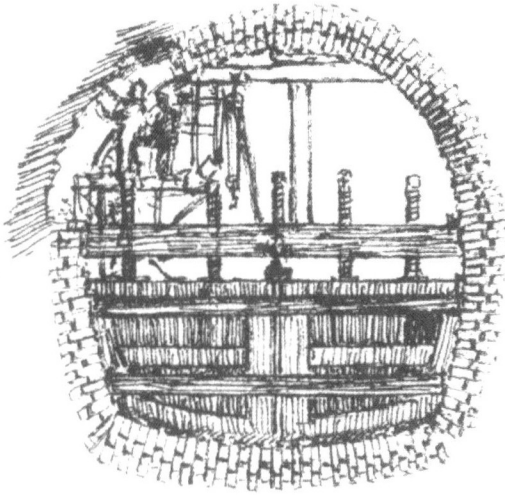

Tunnel maintenance is usually a matter of re-lining the sides, roof or invert; distorted maybe by water pressure, collapsed due to subsidence, rotten with damp or damaged by boats.

The illustration *above* is of a cross section of Blisworth tunnel on the Grand Junction showing the collapse of two thicknesses of brick which occurred in November 1903. To prevent further falls, shoring up was needed which meant closing the tunnel to traffic; so repairs were urgent. This required stanking off the tunnel by cross dams specially designed for the job. Then, as now, repairs could go ahead working from scaffolding erected behind the cross dam.

An unusual aspect of tunnel maintenance was that of soot clearance. The steam tugs that once used the Blisworth and Braunston tunnels gave rise to the need. At first a hawthorn bush was towed through on a boat - but from 1908 a mud boat *below* fitted with three wire brushes conforming to the shape of the tunnel was used. The soot dropped into a forward well.

Ice breaking ends this section on maintenance, as in the same way ice ends traffic movement on a canal. Locks were particularly vulnerable. Floes stuck behind gates, jammed paddle gear, and fouled their openings. In a lock, ice could be broken up by a pounder *opposite top left* or by a flail. Wooden boats were particularly vulnerable to ice damage but could be protected by metal plates *opposite top right* at the stem and along waterlines.

108

While steel boats were safer, no canal boats could make headway against ice of even a few centimetres thick. Narrow ice breaking boats could deal with a maximum of 10cms (4 inches) of ice. These were round bilged, about 10 metres (30-35 feet) long, with longitudinal planking and fully sheathed with metal plates *top right*. A passage was cut by violently rocking the hull - this was achieved by men *above* heaving on a central bar. To avoid broken ice piling up, a channel wider than the ice breaker itself had to be cut. Some ice breakers became motorised but still needed rocking - while larger waterways used tugs such as the "Mayflower", built in 1861 used on the Gloucester and Sharpness Canal.

NEW BEGINNINGS

Canals are perhaps the most enduring of all man made transport systems. In their fundamentals they remain the same as when they were constructed as long as two centuries ago. And yet despite this ability to endure, many have been undergoing often detrimental change from their very outset - and only in recent years can they be seen to be enjoying what amounts to virtual renaissance and redefinition of purpose.

By the late 1800s the waterways were over-shadowed by the railways - in many cases specific routes being taken over by these rivals, and often suffering the consequences of neglect. World War I saw a further decline in their fortunes, with boatmen leaving to join the fighting on the Western Front - and in some cases even boats being commandeered for war duties in France.

Through the interwar years, the waterways struggled on, having to compete with an ever growing number of motor lorries as well as with the established competition from the railways. Despite being nationalised and carrying increased traffic during World War II, the canals' decline continued. Undercapitalised, largely forgotten and with a huge maintenance backlog to be made up, it is no wonder that Tom Rolt in his classic book "Narrow Boat" described the "forlorn and abandoned" waterways that he had travelled along in the early 1940s. But also he saw their charm and potential, and was to become one of the founding fathers of the Inland Waterways Association.

The Inland Waterways Association, founded in 1946, quickly established itself as the major campaigning body for the protection, restoration and use of our waterways, and continues in this role today. Despite the Association's ever increasing membership and influence, many waterways continued to slump into dereliction and disuse during the 1950s. Several preservation victories were won, and campaigning boaters forced their way along neglected routes to maintain navigation rights - but nevertheless some major waterways continued to be lost. It was not until the 1968 Transport Act, which designated specific routes as Cruising Waterways, and the early 1970s when a number of major restoration projects got underway, that the steady decline in the condition and extent of our waterway system was at last checked.

A subsidiary of the Inland Waterways Association - the Waterways Recovery Group - has been of great importance in the restoration movement. Established in 1970, this volunteer group of enthusiasts has provided plant, expertise, experience and labour to underpin the restoration of more than 500 waterway miles.

Using hand tools and muscle power, just like the original navvies, or using more modern machinery such as a Dinkum floating dredger *opposite left*, Waterways Recovery Group volunteers have carried out tasks from the simple clearing of towpaths through to the rebuilding of whole locks.

The diversity of their activities has even included the laying and operation of a narrow gauge railway *top right* along the summit level towpath of the Basingstoke Canal to remove spoil while restoring that navigation. The dredger used - the steam driven "Perseverance" - had previously worked on the restoration of the Kennet and Avon Canal. Illustrated *left* are two pairs of lock gates from the same waterway before, and after such work.

Years of neglect by its railway owners had brought the Kennet and Avon to near unusable condition by 1951 when the last boat struggled along its length. Almost immediately, a Kennet and Avon Association (later to become a Trust) was established. For nearly 40 years, its members worked towards restoration - until some 89 locks - including the magnificent flight of 29 at Caen Hill, Devizes - and many silted up and dry sections (for it has always had problems with water supply) were brought back into use in 1990. The Kennet and Avon Trust is but one of over 80 such canal groups that work to preserve and restore aspects of our waterways heritage. Such groups work in close collaboration with Canal & River Trust, Environment Agency, and Scottish Canals, whose navigations make up the bulk of those in use or under restoration today.

In an urban area, the canal landscape can so easily become just a watery rubbish dump - but in a number of city areas immense progress has been made in recent years in transforming industrial dereliction into an attractive outdoor leisure amenity accessible to all. Illustrated *left* is the view down the Farmers Bridge flight of locks in central Birmingham.

Here, in close proximity to a large convention centre, the modern domed roof of the indoor arena and the telecommunications tower, the contrasting technology of an earlier age has been restored, renewed and given new direction. Two tone brick surfaced towpaths now provide for the walkers, city workers and other escapees from the urban noise and stress who can now find tranquillity while strolling where once cobbles and cinder surfaces provided for working horses. These and similar projects have won a number of conservation awards.

Canals also provide for rural walkers - a 145 mile towpath walk along the route of the Grand Union is one example of such a long distance footpath while increasingly, in an age when wetlands are under threat, canals can also serve as an important ecological asset. A cross section of a waterway provides a diversity of habitats, from the tall vegetation of the hedgerow, across dwarf vegetation which can survive on a towpath, through the emergent vegetation that provides both for bank protection as well as a haven for wild life, into the water itself. The notion of "canal corridors" as providers of linear recreational facilities in addition to being long distance nature reserves, is now well accepted.

Despite two centuries of change and these new objectives, which have emerged from the needs of a post industrial society, our waterways remain strangely unchanged in themselves. Essentially the canal and river are still the province of the boater, walker and the fisherman and no doubt will remain so into the foreseeable future.

TOOLS OF THE TRADE

Our canals were largely built by hand - and even today much of their maintenance depends on using traditional manual skills. By way of a tailpiece, the illustration *opposite* shows a selection of the hand tools as used upon the waterways, drawn from the collection at the National Waterways Museum, Gloucester.

1   Riddle for gunnite, used for pebble dashing wall surfaces - including tunnel linings.

2   Rammer for bedding down masonry.

3   Tool for pressing clay puddle into position.

4   Scoop for sill clearance.

5   Scraper for stop gate groove clearance.

6   Clay spade (from the Lancaster Canal).

7   Two narrow puddling spades.

8   Stretcher for carrying materials.

9   Maul (inscribed CC, believed to be the Coventry Canal).

10   Wrecking axe (from Aire and Calder Navigation).

11   Long handled hammer.

12   Shovel.

13   Adze, for shaping timber.

14   Boring auger, 1.5 inch bit.

15   Corer to obtain soil samples.

16   Carpenter's heavy duty chisels.

17   Draw knives.

18   Plumb line.

19   Mason's lump hammer.

20   Chisels.

21   Pair of Dividers.

22   Mason's maul.

23   Lunch box.

BIBLIOGRAPHY

It is impossible to compile an exhaustive bibliography for a book of this nature; for one thing there is no room, for another Dr Mark Baldwin has already done so in his Canal Books published by himself at Cleobury Mortimer, Shropshire, in 1984. Here however is a reading list, although it must be admitted that many of the titles are somewhat difficult to find.

Notable articles on waterways occur in the Encyclopedia Britannica, in particular in the 3rd edition (1803), 7th edition (1842), 8th edition (1858) and 11th edition (1911).

Of particular relevance to the themes of this work are the following books :-

Burton, A. (1972)
  The Canal Builders* - Eyre Methuen, London.

Chaplin, EH. (1989)
  Waterway Conservation - Whittet Books, London.

Darby, H.C. (1969)
  The Draining of the Fens - University Press, Cambridge.
  First published in 1940 but reprinted in 1969.

deSalis, H.R. (2012)
  Bradshaw's Canals and Navigable Rivers of England and Wales* - Old House Books
  (First edition 1904. Henry Blacklock & Co, London. Reprinted 1969.)

Gladwin, D. (1988)
  Building Britain's Canals* - Brewin Books, Studley.

Hadfield, C. (1950)
  British Canals* - David &. Charles, Newton Abbot.
  First published in 1950 by Phoenix House Ltd and in print ever since with many editions, revised and updated.

Hadfield, C. (1968)
  The Canal Age - David & Charles, Newton Abbot.
  Also published in paperback by Pan Books London, 1971

Harris, R (1969)
  Canals and their Architecture* - Hugh Evelyn, London. (Reprinted since 1969)

Singer, C, Holmyard, E.J., Hall, A.R. and Williams, T.I. (1954-58)
  Oxford History of Technology, Vols III and IV - Clarendon Press, Oxford.

See especially:-
  Doorman, G. - Dredging
  Hadfield, C. - Canals: Inland Waterways of the British Isles

Harris, R. - Land Drainage and Reclamation

Pilkington, R. - Canals: Inland Waterways outside Britain

Skempton, A.W. - Canals and River Navigations before 1750

(Useful information on surveying is to be found in other chapters.)

Paget-Tomlinson, E.W (1978)
The Complete Book of Canal & River Navigations - Waine Research, Wolverhampton.

Paget-Tomlinson, E.W. (1993)
The Illustrated History of Canal & River Navigations* - Academic Press, Sheffield.

Priestley, J. (1969)
Navigable Rivers, Canals and Railways -David & Charles, Newton Abbot. First published in 1831 and reprinted in 1969.

Rees, A. (1972)
Cyclopaedia - David & Charles, Newton Abbot. (First published serially between 1802-20 with the "Canals" section being written by John Farey in 1805. Reprinted in 1972 in five volumes, containing a selection of articles and plates from the original.)

Rolt, L.T.C. (1950)
Inland Waterways of England - Allen & Unwin, London, (re-printed since)

Rolt, L.T.C. (1969)
Navigable Waterways - Longmans, London.

Tew, D. (1984)
Canal Inclines and Lifts - Alan Sutton, Gloucester.

Vernon-Harcourt, L.F. (1896)
Rivers & Canals - Clarendon Press, Oxford. (Two volumes: 1st edition 1882; 2nd edition (enlarged) 1896.)

Wright, I.L. (1977)
Canals in Wales - Bradford Barton, Truro.

The following journal articles also relate:-

"The Anderton Electric Lift" in "The Engineer" July 1908

"The Foxton Inclined Plane" in "Engineering" January 1901

Lewis, M.J.T., Slatcher, W.N. & Jarvis, RN. "Flashlocks on English Waterways: a Survey" in "Industrial Archaeology", Vol 6 No 3. Aug 1969

Lewis, M.J.T., Slatcher, W.N. & Jarvis, RN. "Flashlocks: an Addendum" in Industrial Archaeology, Vol 7 No 2. May 1970

* Current edition available from www.canalbookshop.co.uk

ACKNOWLEDGEMENTS
to first edition 1996

No book is the work of one person, or at any rate no book on a technical subject like this. I am most grateful for outstanding help and encouragement from Roger Hanbury, Environmental and Scientific Services Manager, British Waterways; and from Jonathan Briggs, their Conservation Officer; from Tony Conder, David McDougall and Anne Richards of the National Waterways Museum, Gloucester; David Dutton, Senior Engineer (Reservoirs) British Waterways; Alan Faulkner; Clive Guthrie who took vital photographs; Roger House, formerly Area Engineer, British Waterways at Gloucester; Jane Insley of the Science Museum, South Kensington; Roy Jamieson, Archivist, British Waterways; A. J. Lewery; Robert Ruutel; John Taylor, Water Development Manager, British Waterways; Alan West, formerly on the staff of British Waterways; and Vanessa Wiggins, Media Relations Executive, British Waterways. Ian Wright and his book on the Welsh Canals have also provided much inspiration, as has David Gladwin's "Building Britain's Canals".

I should also like to emphasise the inspiration given by the displays at the National Waterways Museum, Gloucester.

The panoramic illustrations on pages 20 and 27 are based upon Ordnance Survey mapping with the permission of The Controller of HMSO © Crown Copyright.

A special separate thank you must go to Tom Pellow of the Landscape Press who has guided this book through all stages of production and finally brought it to fruition. We agreed that such a work might be useful, combining pictures and text in a fairly light hearted way to inform and enhance the knowledge of the newcomer to the waterways, and to encourage a long lasting commitment.

Edward Paget Tomlinson
Wells, Somerset, 1996

INDEX

Aqueducts, building techniques 40-44, examples 38-45, materials for construction 42-43

Back pumping, 94

Bank protection, 13, 35

Benching - see cutting

Boundary posts, 84

Bridges construction 76, examples 74-82, lift 74, opening 78, swing 81

Broad canal dimensions, 36

Bursts and breaches - see leaks

Bywash, 65

Canal lifts - see lifts

Compensation, weirs and feeders 94

Conservation, waterway value and potential 113

Contour canals, 26-27

Culverts, 37, 56

Cutting canals, 28-33, benching 2, cuttings 33, embankments 33, level sections 29, spoil removal 30, terraces 29, tools used 28

Culverts 37, 56

Drainage, 19

Dredgers, 103

Dredging, needs 100, techniques 102

Embankments, 27, 33, 37

Employees, 98

Flash locks - see locks

Floodgates, 16

Floodbanks, 12

Floods, 19

Gins - see whims

Horse traction, arrangements for 87

Icebreaking, boats and techniques 109

Inclined planes, 66-69

Locks, capacities 90, construction 56-59, early development 15, flash locks 15, flights 54, gates 58-60, locking up and down 52-53, lock keeper accommodation 65, materials for construction 60, paddle gear 62, paired locks 56, pound locks 16, staircases 55, staunches 16, stop locks 59, watergates 15

Lift bridges - see bridges

Lifts, 70-73

Leaks, causes 105, damage from 105, repairs 106, safety precautions 105-106

Maintenance, needs 98, staff 98, yards 99

Mileposts, 84

Mills, dams 11, water needs 11

Narrow canal dimensions, 36

Navigable drains, 19

Paddle gear - see locks

Pegging out route, 36

Planes - see inclined planes

Planning canal route - principles of 22-23

Pound locks - see locks

Puddle, nature of 30, puddle ditches and gutters 31

Pumps, steam 96, water 96, wind 19, 96, electric 97

Recreational value of waterways 113

Reservoirs, construction 91, examples and operation 92-94, siting factors 91

Restoration, 110-112

River navigation improvement, 9-12

Sideponds, 65

Sills and spillways, 65

Sluices, 18

Spoil removal - see cutting

Staunches - see locks

Surveying for route, 21-25

Tools, cutting 28, hand 114

Towpaths, gates 88, maintenance 84, river 9, 88, stiles 88, twin 89, walks 115

Tunnels, building techniques 48, examples 51, maintenance 108, surveying route for 46

Watergates - see locks

Water supply, 90-97

Weirs, feeder 95, fish 11, fixed 18, moveable 18

Whims, horse worked 33